PROPHECY

—— *14 Essential Keys
to Understanding
the Final Drama*

Dr. John F. Walvoord

THOMAS NELSON PUBLISHERS
Nashville

Published in Nashville, Tennessee, by Thomas Nelson, Inc.

Unless otherwise noted, Scripture quotations are from the NEW KING JAMES
VERSION of the Bible. Copyright © 1979, 1980, 1982, Thomas Nelson, Inc.,
Publishers.

Scripture quotations noted NIV are taken from the HOLY BIBLE, NEW
INTERNATIONAL VERSION ®. Copyright © 1973, 1978, 1984 by International
Bible Society. Used by permission of Zondervan Bible Publishing House. All
rights reserved. The "NIV" and "New International Version" trademarks are
registered in the United States Patent and Trademark Office by
International Bible Society. Use of either trademark requires the permission
of International Bible Society.

Scripture quotations noted KJV are from *The Holy Bible*, KING JAMES VERSION.

Library of Congress Cataloging-in-Publication Data

Walvoord, John F.
    Prophecy : 14 essential keys to understanding the final drama / John F.
Walvoord.
        p.   cm.
    Includes indexes.
    ISBN 0-8407-3434-4
    1. Bible—Prophecies. 2. Eschatology. 3. World politics—1985–1995.
I. Title.
BS647.2.W334   1993
220.1'5—dc20
                                                                92–44728
                                                                CIP

Printed in the United States of America

2 3 4 5 6 7 - 98 97 96 95 94 93

Contents

Acknowledgments

The excellent work of Karen Grassmick as stenographer for this volume did much to bring this book to acceptable publishing standards.

Introduction

Many have been shaken by the tremendous events of this last decade of the twentieth century. The Iraqi invasion of Kuwait brought the world to attention because of the importance of Middle Eastern oil. The response of thirty nations to turn back the Iraqi army and drive it out of Kuwait was the first time in history that such a united effort resulted in military action in the Middle East. The fact that so many prophecies of the Bible pertain to that part of the world immediately raised the question of whether these events indicated the consummation of the age, the approach to the battle of Armageddon, and the Second Coming.

As a resolution of the Middle East crisis began, however, it became evident that these events were not precisely the fulfillment of what the Bible predicts for the future. Instead they could be a setting of the stage for the final drama leading to the Second Coming. The result was a renewed interest in prophecy and questions arose concerning what can be believed about biblical prophecy. Even the secular press paid close attention to the prophetic significance of the Middle East crisis and indulged in speculation as to how it relates to the Bible. Although the events sparked some premature conclusions that the world is already in the end time, they had a beneficial effect on the study of prophecy. Many people searched the Scriptures, some perhaps for the first time, to learn what the Bible says about the end of the age.

The twentieth century has witnessed tremendous strides in the study of theology as a whole, as well as the study of prophecy. The investigations have focused on a number of important doctrines. The liberal versus fundamentalist controversy in the church in the 1920s resulted in wide divisions and the establishment of new denominations. Attention has been focused on the question of the inerrancy of the Bible and the doctrine of creation as opposed to natural evolution. The rise of the Pentecostal movement, with its emphasis on the ministry of the Holy Spirit, is a primary characteristic of the twentieth century.

In a century during which there has been rapid progress scientifically and intellectually, it was natural for renewed study of eschatology to occur. Accordingly, the twentieth century has witnessed a number of important treatments of the subject of prophecy, both on the level of highest scholarship and in books designed for popular reading. Attention has focused on major issues, such as the doctrine of the millennium, and the questions have included:

Will the Second Coming precede the millennium, the thousand-year kingdom predicted in the Bible?

A view known as *premillennialism* concludes that it will.

Will prophecy of the millennial kingdom be fulfilled only in a nonliteral way, and will it take place in the present age?

The doctrine of the millennium known as *amillennialism* is the view that has characterized much of the church. Most of those who hold this viewpoint believe that when Christ returns, this second coming will immediately usher in the new heaven and new earth and the eternal state.

Will the world get better and better and more Christianized through preaching the Gospel until it reaches a thousand years of a golden age, with Christ coming at the end of the period?

This viewpoint, known as *postmillennialism*, was popular in the nineteenth century and still finds favor with a good many theologians.

Obviously these three views offer radically different

proposals regarding future events. In general, the twentieth century has been a time of decline for postmillennialism, but there has been a rise in both premillennialism and amillennialism. (For further discussion see chapters 1, 11, and 12.)

During this last decade of the twentieth century, the focus is on prophecy. Disturbances in the Middle East, the war in Iraq and Kuwait, unsettled conditions in the Soviet Union, and questions of how these events fit into the prophetic scheme have occupied both the secular and religious press. Although there is general agreement that the events which have transpired are not specific fulfillment of prophecy, nevertheless they fit into the framework of prophecy as it is portrayed in Scripture for the end of the age. Even the secular press is aware of the fact that Christ said He who came once, as recorded in history, has promised to return to the Mount of Olives. There is general awareness that this is connected with judgment on sin and on a world which has largely rejected Christ. Accordingly, questions have arisen as to how current events fit into all this and what the timetable is for end-time events.

In this context, reviewing the essentials of prophecy is important. About one-fourth of the Bible is predictive prophecy. About half of these prophecies have already been fulfilled very literally. This leads to the conclusion that prophecies yet to be fulfilled will have the same kind of literal fulfillment. Therefore, a study of the prophecy concerning events of the past will give many guidelines for understanding the fulfillment of the prophecy of events in the future. Included in such a study and of preeminent interest to Christians are prophecy and its fulfillment regarding Jesus Christ. His coming is predicted all through the Old Testament. The New Testament describes how those prophecies were fulfilled and includes prophecies concerning a second coming that are not yet fulfilled (see chapter 11). In many respects the Second Coming dominates the prophetic scene for those who have put their trust in Christ.

General prophecies recorded in the Bible in the early chapters of Genesis lay the foundation for human history. The book of Daniel predicts seven great world empires. Six of them have already arisen and the prophecies have been almost entirely fulfilled. The seventh empire is the kingdom of God that will come from heaven at the Second Coming (see chapters 4 and 12). Along with prophecies concerning the human race are those relating to Satan and the demonic world. This brings up the difficult question often raised philosophically concerning the origin of evil in a world that is governed by a good God. The Scriptures reveal much concerning Satan's program in the past, his present activities, and the way God will judge him (see chapter 5).

In prophecy Israel is one of the major doctrines of the Bible, beginning in Genesis and continuing throughout Scripture (see chapter 6). Important in the history and prophecy of Israel are the great covenants of God, such as the Abrahamic Covenant, the Palestinian Covenant, the Davidic Covenant, and the New Covenant (see chapters 3 and 6). Many promises involved in predictive prophecy concerning Israel have already been fulfilled, but according to the Bible, the nation still has a glorious future ahead.

Prophecies for the church in the present age are a major doctrine of Scripture that Christ introduced in the Upper Room (see John 13–17). They were revealed in the New Testament and have been partially fulfilled in the present age (see chapter 7). One of the keys to understanding prophecy is learning to distinguish carefully what the Bible has to say about the future of Israel, about the future of the church, and about the future of the world. Prophecy reveals the intermediate state where people go who die and describes their state before their resurrection (see chapter 8). Prophecy has its grand consummation in the doctrines of heaven, the rapture of the church—followed by the great time of trouble at the end (the great tribulation), the second coming of Christ, the millennial kingdom—the thousand-year reign of Christ, and ultimately eternity, involving eternal punishment for the lost and dwelling in the new Jerusalem in the new heaven and new earth for those who are saved. In the final judgments all moral creatures, whether satanic or holy angels or human beings, will be judged and allotted their eternal destinies (see chapters 9, 10, 11, 13, and 14). Obviously the future outcome of our present history should be a subject of great concern and interest on the part of everyone who is thinking about ultimate matters.

This work attempts to state succinctly the major elements that relate to the prophetic future. The outline of future events provided here forms a fitting platform on which to explore in-depth the Bible's detailed prophecies. After all, Christianity without prophecy would be an existence without hope. Evidently God intended that we understand the contents of the prophetic Word and that it would have a bearing upon the practical decisions Christians make. On one hand, we should pay careful attention to the Scriptures to determine exactly what they predict. But on the other hand, we must avoid the tendency to incorporate man's speculations into prophecy.

This work is offered in the hope of providing a clearer picture of the future for those who were confused by previous studies. It is also offered in the hope that this introduction will serve as a foundation on which future, more in-depth study of the prophecies of Scripture can be undertaken. In it all, may Christ be glorified and Christians challenged to faith and commitment in response to what the future holds.

— 1 —

THE FIRST KEY

Interpreting Correctly

Prophecy is the doctrine of Scripture dealing with predictions of events that will occur in the future. Theologians call this doctrine *eschatology*, a word derived from the Greek *eschatos*, meaning "last" or "last things." It refers to the events that will climax human history. Included in biblical eschatology are all predictions that were future at the time they were written, whether they have been fulfilled now or are still unfulfilled.

Key prophecies in Scripture deal with the whole scope of world history and include many important events. These include divine purposes for the nation of Israel, prophecies relating to the first and second comings of Jesus Christ, the course and destiny of the church, and the consummation of human history in a kingdom on earth. Involved are such subjects as salvation, death and resurrection, divine judgments of men, angels and demons, eternal punishment, heaven, the New Jerusalem, and the new heaven and new earth.

Basic Principles of Biblical Interpretation
Premises and Assumptions

No area of theology has had more widespread differences in interpretation than the doctrine of prophecy. This is partly because some fulfillment is still in the future and there is the possibility of differing interpretations of what the unfulfilled prophecies actually mean. In the study of Scripture, however, there are certain well-established principles of interpretation that guide the one who attempts to understand the Bible. These principles are keys to comprehending prophecy clearly and must be kept in mind when any portion of Scripture, especially prophecy, is being interpreted.

There are certain premises and assumptions, beliefs that are basic indisputable truths—things which are taken as true, that help guide prophecy interpretation. Four of these assumptions are vitally important and must be recognized and fully embraced before correct scriptural interpretation is possible.

God is sovereign.

Eschatology assumes that God is sovereign and is directing the course of human history toward an intelligent end. Therefore, the fulfillment of prophecy is the realization of God's sovereign purposes. Inherent in the fulfillment are the elements of human choice, divine influence, natural law, and God's supernatural intervention.

Although God is sovereign in His guidance of mankind, He allows human choice. In creation God gave man a will. With this will man can make choices between alternatives. This is a common fact of human experience and is recognized throughout the Bible. For instance, in John 7:17 Christ says, "If anyone chooses to do God's will, he will find out whether my teaching comes from God or whether I speak on my own" (NIV). Man is able to choose whether or not he will serve God and whether or not he believes in Christ. There is, of course, divine influence, especially for Christians. According to Philippians 2:13, "It is God who works in you both to will and to do for His good pleasure."

Natural law is also an integral part of the human experience, for we must obey the law of gravity and other physical laws that are inherent in nature. In the Christian faith, however, there is also the matter of God's supernatural intervention. This is involved in our salvation, in answer to prayer, in God's protection, and in God's opening to us knowledge of Scripture. By its nature Christianity is supernatural.

All these forms of fulfilling the purposes of God are involved in what is called *providence*, the doctrine that God directs all events in keeping with His sovereign will.

God is omniscient.

Intrinsic in eschatology is the concept that God knows all things. His knowledge extends not only to things that will occur in the future, but also to all things that will not occur. Accordingly, His omniscience includes everything and all the possibilities of every event. Acts 15:18 says, "Known to God from eternity are all His works." In Isaiah 46:10 we find God speaking to us through His prophet Isaiah, saying, "I make known the end from the beginning, from ancient times, what is still to come" (NIV). Because God is omniscient, He knows all things: "And there is no creature hidden from His sight, but all things are naked and open to the eyes of Him to whom we must give account" (Heb. 4:13).

Foreknowledge means God knows what will actually happen. He knows the future in all its detail as clearly as He knows history or prophecies already fulfilled. No fact of the future, however minute, is outside His knowledge. Still, prophecy does not reveal everything about the future, nor does it fully reveal all of God's intentions.

Biblical revelation is accurate.

Eschatology is based on the fact that God supernaturally inspired the Bible and that the revelation of prophecy recorded in Scripture is divinely accurate. Obviously if the Bible were not inspired and were merely the work of men, it would contain many errors and its prophecies about the future would be merely intelligent guesses. We know the Bible is divinely inspired because the literal fulfillment of about 50 percent of its prophecies demonstrates that biblical prophecy is accurate. No other book in all the world has a record like this.

Prophecy is also credible because the Bible contains evidence that it was inspired by God and He directed its writing. Although they were fallible men, the writers of Scripture recorded without error what God directed them to write. A part of the evidence is found in Matthew 5:17 – 18, where Christ states, "Do not think that I came to destroy the Law or the Prophets. I did not come to destroy but to fulfill. For assuredly, I say to you, till heaven and earth pass away, one jot or one tittle will by no means pass from the law till all is fulfilled."

Revelation 22:18–19 gives a solemn warning about the failure to recognize the accuracy of prophecy: "For I testify to everyone who hears the words of the prophecy of this book: If anyone adds to these things, God will add to him the plagues that are written in this book; and if anyone takes away from the words of the book of this prophecy, God shall take away his part from the Book of Life, from the holy city, and from the things which are written in this book." We can assume that biblical prophecy is as errorless as any other portion of Scripture, even though the writers expressed concepts and predicted future events that were beyond their knowledge.

Inspiration does not mean that God dictated the entire Scripture. He allowed men the freedom to write, but at the same time He guided them so that they made no mistakes. They incorporated what He had revealed to them supernaturally. As the Bible makes clear, God allowed the writers to express their own opinions, their own feelings, their own hopes, and their own fears. In each case God allowed them to state accurately normative human experience. With prophecy, however, obviously the writers went beyond their own experiences, as well as their feelings and hopes. This is the meaning of 2 Peter 1:20–21: "Above all, you must understand that no prophecy of Scripture came about by the prophet's own interpretation. For prophecy never had its origin in the will of man, but men spoke from God as they were carried along by the Holy Spirit" (NIV). Eschatology in any systematic form would be impossible apart from the authoritative and accurate predictions of Scripture.

Prophecy is understandable.

A basic foundational principle of eschatology is that prophecy can be understood. While many prophetic portions of Scripture may not be completely clear until after they are fulfilled, their incorporation in God's Word can be taken as the expression of His divine intention that the reader can understand the prophetic program they reveal.

Accordingly, while the details may not always be understandable, the broad purposes of the predictions can be understood, especially with the guidance and illumination of the Holy Spirit. The notion that prophecy cannot be understood and that it presents a hopeless enigma to human intelligence must, therefore, be rejected.

The Basics Applied to Eschatology

One of the major problems of interpreting eschatology is deciding if prophecy should be interpreted literally or non-literally. In orthodox theology the general principle of literal interpretation, often called the grammatical-historical method, is assumed to be correct and the only method giving a true interpretation of Scripture. In the literal method, the words of Scripture are understood as indicated by the context in their ordinary, normal, customary usage. This method recognizes that figurative language is frequently found in Scripture and that it always provides an understandable truth. Even though a figure is used, the passage teaches a literal truth. For example, Christ stated, "I am the true vine, and My Father is the vinedresser" (John 15:1). Throughout this figure, He spoke of people as branches and mentioned the fruit they bear. Christ was not literally a vine. However, the literal truth of the figure is clearly understandable. Some books of the Bible, Ezekiel and Revelation, for example, contain many passages incorporating figurative language. The concept of the literal method is that while occasionally allegory and figurative language are used in Scripture, these instances are plainly indicated and can be interpreted alongside other portions which are clearly literal.

In contrast to the literal method, the allegorical method tries to interpret the words of Scripture in a secondary sense. The basis of this method is that the truth being taught is something other than the literal and historical meaning. This opens the way for the interpreter to read into the words of Scripture whatever fanciful meaning might seem to him to be appropriate.

Is Eschatology a Special Case?

Although orthodox interpreters of the Bible generally reject allegorical and figurative interpretation of Scripture, the theory has been advanced that eschatology is a special case. Some believe we should not attempt to understand scriptural prophecy literally, especially when such literal interpretation would contradict the presuppositions of the interpreter.

The question of whether to interpret Scripture literally as opposed to non-literally is, therefore, a major controversy in the study of eschatology. Any student of prophetic Scripture must decide early whether prophecy should normally be understood by its literal meaning or in another way.

Historically the literal interpretation of eschatology led to premillennialism, the view that Christ's second coming will be followed by His reign over an earthly kingdom for one thousand years. In contrast, non-literal interpretation led to amillennialism, the system of interpretation that denies there will be a thousand-year kingdom after the Second Coming. Non-literal interpretation also has tended to support postmillennialism, the position that a golden age on earth of one thousand years will precede Christ's second coming.

It is generally agreed that the major divisions of eschatology into premillennial, amillennial, and postmillennial interpretations are derived from differences in the theory and application of literal interpretation of prophecy.

Old Testament Prophecy

Conservatives generally interpret literally the Old Tes-

tament prophecies relating to such important subjects as
the coming of Christ and the future life, prophecies concerning the nations, and prophecies concerning Israel that
were fulfilled in the Old Testament period. Significant
differences arise in interpreting the predictions of a future
kingdom.

Premillenarians believe prophecies of the future kingdom indicate a reign of Christ on earth after His second
coming. They hold that the prophecies relating to the
period following Christ's second coming will be fulfilled
just as literally as the prophecies concerning His first
coming. They interpret the kingdom prophecies to mean
there will literally be a kingdom on earth lasting one
thousand years, during which time Christ will reign as
King of kings and Lord of lords.

Amillenarians advocate a belief that the future kingdom prophecies will be fulfilled, *but* they offer alternative
methods of interpretation based on four separate and
distinct assumptions about biblical prophecy: (1) The
kingdom promises should be interpreted non-literally;
they actually refer to Christ's reigning in the hearts of
believers. (2) The prophecies are literal, but conditional;
the conditions have not been met; therefore, the prophecies will not be fulfilled. (3) The prophecies will be fulfilled
non-literally either in the intermediate state before resurrection or in heaven. (4) The millennium will be fulfilled
in the eternal state in the new Jerusalem.

Postmillenarians' interpretation of the kingdom prophecies is that they will be fulfilled during the last one thousand
years of the present age. According to their view, during
this time the Gospel will be triumphant and the earthly
kingdom will conclude with the Second Coming.

New Testament Prophecy

Because many of the promises concerning an earthly
kingdom are not repeated in the New Testament,
amillenarians say that confirms their interpretation of the
Old Testament and leads them to believe the kingdom

promises will not be fulfilled literally. Premillenarians argue this is not true and point to certain Old Testament prophecies that are confirmed in the New Testament. For example, in the angel's announcement of the virgin birth of the Messiah to Mary, which is recorded in Luke, Gabriel promised Mary that her son would be given the throne of David and would reign over Israel forever. He said, "Do not be afraid, Mary, for you have found favor with God. And behold, you will conceive in your womb and bring forth a Son, and shall call His name JESUS. He will be great, and will be called the Son of the Highest; and the Lord God will give Him the throne of His father David. And He will reign over the house of Jacob forever, and of His kingdom there will be no end" (Luke 1:30–33). Based on Old Testament prophecy, the common Jewish expectation was that when the Messiah came, He would establish an earthly kingdom. Therefore, Mary would naturally interpret the angel's promise as confirming this commonly held expectation. If her hope had proved to be wrong, the angel's promise would have amounted to a deception. But Mary was not deceived. She was, however, mistaken in her belief that the Messiah's birth and the earthly kingdom would be parts of the same event.

The disciples also anticipated an earthly kingdom during Jesus' earthly ministry. This is revealed by the mother of James and John asking for special consideration for her sons in the kingdom. Matthew records Jesus' response in which He explained it was not yet time for His kingdom.

Then the mother of Zebedee's sons came to Him with her sons, kneeling down and asking something from Him. And He said to her, "What do you wish?" She said to Him, "Grant that these two sons of mine may sit, one on Your right hand and the other on the left, in Your kingdom."

But Jesus answered and said, "You do not know what you ask. Are you able to drink the cup that I am about to drink, and be baptized with the baptism that I am baptized with?" They said to Him, "We are able." So He said to them, "You will indeed drink My cup, and be baptized with the baptism that I am baptized with; but to sit on My right hand and on My left is not Mine to give, but it is for those for whom it is prepared by My Father." (Matt. 20:20–23)

Christ also promised the disciples they would sit on thrones judging the twelve tribes of Israel in the kingdom, saying "And I bestow upon you a kingdom, just as My Father bestowed one upon Me, that you may eat and drink at My table in My kingdom, and sit on thrones judging the twelve tribes of Israel" (Luke 22:29–30).

At the end of Christ's earthly life, the disciples were still asking when the new kingdom would be established. We read in Acts: "Therefore, when they had come together, they asked Him, saying, 'Lord, will You at this time restore the kingdom to Israel?' And He said to them, 'It is not for you to know times or seasons which the Father has put in His own authority'" (Acts 1:6–7). In answering their question, Christ did not tell the disciples they had misunderstood, but only that they could not know the time. He confirmed that a portion of the Old Testament prophecy had been fulfilled and the remainder would happen in the future.

The apostle Paul considers the confusion over Israel's promises in Romans 9–11, where he emphatically denies the possibility that God might not fulfill His promises, saying, "God forbid" (Rom. 11:1 KJV). Paul predicted that Israel as a nation would be delivered at the time of the Second Coming, when, drawing from Old Testament prophecy, he wrote: "For I do not desire, brethren, that you should be ignorant of this mystery, lest you should be wise in your own opinion, that hardening in part has happened to Israel until the fullness of the Gentiles has come in. And so all Israel will be saved, as it is written:

"The Deliverer will come out of Zion,
And He will turn away ungodliness from Jacob;
For this is My covenant with them,
When I take away their sins." (Rom. 11:25–27)

In the book of Revelation, the apostle John affirms six times that Christ will reign for one thousand years (20:2–7) after binding Satan (vv. 1–3) and judging the wicked who are living on earth at that time (Ezek. 20:33–38; Matt. 25:31–46; Rev. 19:17–21). At the end of the thousand years the wicked dead will rise and be judged (Rev. 20:11–15). We must all agree that if Revelation 20 is interpreted literally, it teaches that Christ will reign over an earthly kingdom.

One of the most significant facts revealed by the New Testament is that during the first century there was complete agreement about this teaching of a coming earthly kingdom. All agree this was common Jewish expectation. If it had been a vain hope, extensive corrective teaching would have been required. Even amillenarians agree that if the Bible is interpreted literally, the premillennial understanding of the coming kingdom is the only possible interpretation.

Those who interpret the New Testament conservatively, while differing on the specifics of a future millennium, do agree on the great central doctrines of the Christian faith, such as the certainty of the resurrection and judgment of all men, the doctrine of the future life—including eternal blessing for the saved and eternal punishment for the lost, and the literal fulfillment of prophecies relating to these doctrines.

Modern liberal theologians have challenged this interpretation and suggest either conditional immortality (only the righteous will be resurrected) or universalism (eventually all will be saved). The liberals have often questioned the literalness of resurrection and divine judgment and especially the revelation of everlasting punishment. Conservative theology has rejected these denials of the ultimate fulfillment of prophecy. All who accept the Bible as the inspired Word of God agree the Christian hope is eternal and fulfillment of the prophecies is certain.

For the most part, the ancient church followed the teachings of the Apostles in the first few centuries after Christ's earthly life ended. Those who were considered orthodox accepted without question biblical teachings concerning resurrection, divine judgment on sin, the truth of

the Second Coming, and the everlasting character of
human existence for both the righteous and the unrighteous. In the first two centuries there seems to have been
no controversy on whether Christ would reign on earth
after His second coming. Evidence which has been pre-
served indicates that it was the common hope of the
Church that Christ would return and reign on earth.

In keeping with the total lack of positive evidence for
amillennialism in the first two centuries, early fathers,
such as Pothinus, Justin Martyr, Melito, Hegesippus,
Tatian, Irenaeus, Tertullian, Hippolytus, and Apollinaris,
all seem to have been premillennial.

The Rise of Amillennialism

In the history of the early church, premillennialism
began its decline and amillennialism began its rise at the
close of the second and the beginning of the third centuries
of the Christian era. Opponents of premillennialism from
a school of theology at Alexandria, Egypt, proposed that
Scripture should be interpreted non-literally. Their leaders were Gaius, Clement of Alexandria, Origen, and Dio-
nysius. Today practically all conservative expositors
regard these men as heretics, not only because they attacked premillennialism, but because they also attacked
most orthodox doctrines of theology. Others, who maintained a literal interpretation of prophecy, opposed this
point of view; some of these were Cyprian, Commodian,
Nepos, Coracion, Victorinus, Methodius, and Lactantius.
However, the Alexandrian school of theology managed to
extend its teaching across Northern Africa and more than
a century later this interpretation influenced the great
theologian Augustine. Beginning in the third century, the
controversy over literal versus non-literal prophetic interpretation became prominent.

Modern amillennialism owes its major impetus to Augustine, the Roman Catholic bishop of Hippo in Northern Africa
(354–430). Augustine discarded many of what he considered objectionable features of the Alexandrian non-literal
interpretation. Subsequently he developed a form of inter-

pretation that regards all of the Bible as subject to literal interpretation, but with prophecy of the millennium a major exception. Accordingly, while following many orthodox doctrines of Scripture, Augustine rejected the idea of a literal millennial kingdom. His interpretations had great influence on the theology of the Roman Catholic Church developed later. Protestant Reformers of the sixteenth century widely adopted his view also.

Augustine believed the age in which he lived spiritually fulfilled the concept of a kingdom on earth, which would climax in the second coming of Christ, judgment of the wicked, and rewarding of the blessed. However, protestantism later refined, in part, Roman Catholic eschatology by discarding the doctrine of purgatory and affirming other great doctrines of the Protestant Reformation.

AMILLENNIAL CHART OF THE FUTURE
AUGUSTINIAN VIEW

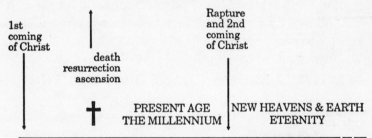

The Rise of Postmillennialism

Daniel Whitby (1638–1725) developed a variation of amillennialism, usually called postmillennialism, in the seventeenth century. While earlier others held similar views, Whitby popularized the concept that the world would grow progressively better until it climaxed in a golden age of one thousand years during which the Gospel would be triumphant. This earthly millennial kingdom would conclude with the second coming of Christ, a postmillennial event.

Many conservative theologians of the eighteenth and nineteenth centuries adopted postmillennialism. With the rise of evolution, it also appealed to liberals who saw in its optimism the biblical counterpart to the concept of evolutionary development. With the coming of the twentieth century and its two great world wars, however, the optimism of postmillennialism largely dissipated, and conservative interpreters were primarily premillenarians and amillenarians.

Contemporary Interpretation

In the twentieth century eschatology is divided into three major sections: (1) the premillennial stance held by those who interpret prophecy literally; (2) the conservative amillennial stance, held by those who affirm a literal future life, including heaven and hell, divine judgment on the righteous and the wicked, and the doctrine of the resurrection of all men, but reject a literal millennial kingdom; and (3) the liberal postmillennial stance which, while allowing for a future life, tends to deny judgment on the wicked and rejects the literal resurrection of the body and the actual second coming of Christ.

POSTMILLENNIAL CHART OF THE FUTURE

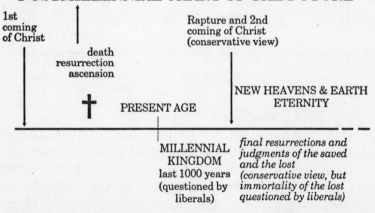

Contemporary eschatology, accordingly, hinges on the question of whether the Bible is what it claims to be, the inspired Word of God, and, therefore, is authoritative in prophecy and in history and constitutes an accurate, divine revelation. Those accepting the Bible as inspired continue to be divided on the issue of whether prophecy should be interpreted literally or non-literally. Those choosing a literal interpretation are almost invariably premillenarian. The opinions of those adhering to a non-literal interpretation vary widely and normally deny a future millennium. They are, therefore, classified as amillennial, as are those who reject inspiration.

At the outset of any attempt to interpret the prophecies of the Bible, the interpreter faces two decisions: whether or not he believes the Bible is inspired and what method of interpretation he will follow. The literal interpretation of prophecy provides some uniformity in agreement among those who follow this method, but the non-literal method turns the interpreter loose on the broad sea of varying opinions which usually involve a measure of unbelief as to any specific program of future events. Accordingly, for those who reject the literal interpretation of prophecy, it is almost impossible to find any areas of major agreement. The adherents of the non-literal method usually turn away from eschatology as a major area of theological study.

PREMILLENNIAL CHART OF THE FUTURE
PRETRIBULATIONAL VIEW

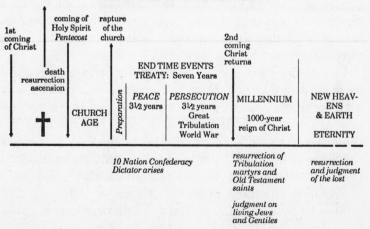

2

THE SECOND KEY

Jesus Christ

Theologians have often pointed out that Jesus Christ is the center of theology because all the great purposes of God depend on Him—His person and His works. What is true of theology as a whole is especially true of eschatology. Biblical prophecies about Jesus Christ begin in Genesis with the Garden of Eden and climax in the last book of the Bible, with its theme "The Revelation of Jesus Christ" (Rev. 1:1). Accordingly, while prophecy in its broad revelation deals with such great scenes as the history of the world, the divine program of God for Israel, and His plan for the church, central in all these great themes is Jesus Christ, the Savior, the ultimate judge of all men, the final victor over sin and death. All prophecy, whatever its theme, is ultimately connected in some way or other to the purposes of God in and through Christ.

Prophecies concerning Jesus Christ form a major link between the Old and New Testaments. The Old Testament predicts Jesus Christ as Savior, and those prophecies are largely fulfilled in the New Testament. The themes and unfulfilled prophecies of the Old Testament continue in the New by way of fulfillment and additional predictions that have not yet been fulfilled.

Probably the most dominant theme of prophecy as it relates to Jesus Christ is God's divine program of salvation. In divine dealings with the world, we see Christ as the sovereign judge who guides history to its intelligent end. God's purpose is that every knee should bow to Him (Rom. 14:11) and that Christ is the ultimate victor over Satan, sin, and death (1 Cor. 15:24–28). Consistent with Christ's central place in prophecy are details concerning His person and work in both the Old and New Testaments that are largely related to two foci—His first coming and His second coming. These predictions reveal not only the events, but also His character and majesty.

The First Coming of Christ

The first coming of Christ is repeatedly a subject of the major books of the Old Testament. Beginning with the introduction of Christ as the "offspring" of Eve (Gen. 3:15 NIV) in anticipation of the virgin birth, major passages deal with Christ's place in the prophetic program. Accordingly, in the Old Testament Christ is essential to God's promise to Abraham: "And in you all the families of the earth shall be blessed" (Gen. 12:3). The Messiah would be a descendant of Isaac (Gen. 17:19) and linked to the line of Jacob (Gen. 28:14). Prophecy said He would come as the king from Judah: "The scepter shall not depart from Judah, nor a lawgiver from between his feet, until Shiloh comes" (Gen. 49:10).

Psalm 110:4 predicts Christ's priesthood: "You are a priest forever / According to the order of Melchizedek." He would be a prophet like Moses: "The LORD your God will raise up for you a prophet like me from your midst, from your brethren. Him you shall hear. . . . And the LORD said . . . 'I will raise up for them a Prophet like you from among their brethren, and will put My words in His mouth, and He shall speak to them all that I command Him' " (Deut. 18:15, 17–18).

These prophecies indicate that Christ would be a descendant of David (2 Sam. 7:12–16). In making this covenant with David, God said, "And your house and your kingdom shall be established forever before you. Your throne shall be established forever" (v. 16). He would also be the king who would fulfill God's promise to David that

one in his lineage would reign forever (2 Sam. 7:16; Ps.
2:4 – 5; 72; 110; Isa. 9:6 – 7; Dan. 7:13 – 14; Micah 5:2;
Zech. 9:9).

The Psalms reveal much concerning Christ, including
His ultimate triumph (Ps. 2:6–9). The Lord said, "Yet I
have set My King/On My holy hill of Zion" (Ps. 2:6). Psalm
16:10 predicts His resurrection: "For You will not leave
my soul in Sheol, / Nor will You allow Your Holy One to
see corruption." Psalm 22:1–18 describes Christ's death
with the very words He spoke later on the cross stated in
verse 1. Many passages, including all of Psalm 72, are
devoted to His millennial reign with Psalm 89 mentioning
throughout that His reign will be the fulfillment of the
Davidic Covenant.

Isaiah 7:14 predicts His virgin birth: "Therefore the
Lord Himself will give you a sign: Behold, the virgin shall
conceive and bear a Son, and shall call His name Immanuel." Isaiah 9:6–7 adds:

> For unto us a Child is born,
> Unto us a Son is given;
> And the government will be upon His shoulder.
> And His name will be called
> Wonderful, Counselor, Mighty God,
> Everlasting Father, Prince of Peace.
> Of the increase of His government and peace
> There will be no end,
> Upon the throne of David and over His kingdom,
> To order it and establish it with judgment and justice
> From that time forward, even forever.
> The zeal of the LORD of hosts will perform this.

Isaiah 42:1–7 describes His ministry to man in His first
coming.

Many passages predict His humiliation and death
(50:4–7; 52:13–53:12). These Isaiah passages need to be
studied in detail as they picture Christ's humiliation, His
suffering on the cross, the piercing of His hands and feet,
and the fact that "All we like sheep have gone astray; / We
have turned, every one, to his own way; / And the LORD
has laid on Him the iniquity of us all" (Isa. 53:6). His

crucifixion, likened to a lamb being led to slaughter, His death with the wicked, and His grave with the rich are all detailed in this passage. It concludes with verse 12:

Therefore I will divide Him a portion with the great,
And He shall divide the spoil with the strong,
Because He poured out His soul unto death,
And He was numbered with the transgressors,
And He bore the sin of many,
And made intercession for the transgressors.

The Spirit of God will be upon Him (61:1) as Christ Himself quoted in Luke 4:16–19.

Daniel speaks of the Son of God's first coming and death (9:25–26), referring to Christ as "the Messiah" or "the Anointed One" (NIV) who "will be cut off and will have nothing" (referring to His death, NIV). An outstanding illustration of literal fulfillment of prophecy is Micah's prediction that Christ would be born in Bethlehem:

But you, Bethlehem Ephrathah,
Though you are little among the thousands of Judah,
Yet out of you shall come forth to Me
The One to be ruler in Israel,
Whose goings forth have been from of old,
From everlasting.   (Micah 5:2)

Zechariah predicted His coming to Israel as their King:

Rejoice greatly, O daughter of Zion!
Shout, O daughter of Jerusalem!
Behold, your King is coming to you;
He is just and having salvation,
Lowly and riding on a donkey,
A colt, the foal of a donkey.   (Zech. 9:9)

This passage describes Christ's triumphal entry into Jerusalem shortly before His death. This, again, is a marvelous illustration of the literal fulfillment of prophecy.

Zechariah graphically predicted Judas' betrayal: "Then I said to them, 'If it is agreeable to you, give me my wages; and if not, refrain.' So they weighed out for my wages thirty pieces of silver. And the LORD said to me, ' Throw it to the potter'—that princely price they set on me. So I took the thirty pieces of silver and threw them into the house

of the LORD for the potter" (11:12–13). Verses 13:6–7
describe Christ's death, and Malachi predicted the coming
of John the Baptist as the messenger (Mal. 3:1; Matt.
11:10; Mark 1:2; Luke 7:27).

Old Testament Prophecy Fulfilled in the New Testament

The Old Testament predictions of the first coming are
fulfilled in the New Testament as Christ's life, ministry,
death, and resurrection unfold (Matt. 1:1–17; 2:1–6; 4:15–
16; 12:18–21; 21:1–5, 42–44; 26:31; 27:9–10, 35, 46, 50;
28:5–6; with many additional references in Mark, Luke,
and John), and climax in His ascension into heaven (Acts
1:9).

The Birth of Jesus Christ

As early as Genesis 3:15, we find prophecies of the birth
of Jesus Christ, which can be traced through the Old
Testament in the narrowing line of the Messiah through
Seth (Gen. 4:26), Noah, and Noah's son, Shem (10:1). The
line continues through Abraham (12:3), Isaac, and Jacob
(26:3; 28:14). The Savior would be from the tribe of Judah
(49:10) and the house of David (2 Sam. 7:12–16).

In the New Testament period it was clearly revealed
that Christ descended from Nathan, a son of David, rather
than from Solomon (Luke 3:31). This is in keeping with
the curse placed upon the descendants of Solomon because
of the sin of Jehoiakim, king of Judah, who burned the
prophecies of Jeremiah (Jer. 36:29–31): "Therefore thus
says the LORD concerning Jehoiakim king of Judah: 'He
shall have no one to sit on the throne of David, and his
dead body shall be cast out to the heat of the day and the
frost of the night' " (v. 30).

Earlier, in Jeremiah 22:30, the Lord denounced
Jehoiachin, who was the son of Jehoiakim:

Thus says the LORD:
"Write this man down as childless,
A man who shall not prosper in his days;
For none of his descendants shall prosper,

Sitting on the throne of David,
And ruling anymore in Judah."

Actually, Jehoiachin's children sat on the throne briefly, but clearly his descendants were cursed as far as remaining on the throne is concerned. This prophecy also confirms the virgin birth of Christ. Joseph, Mary's husband, was a descendant of Jehoiakim and his son Jehoiachin, who is referred to in Matthew 1:11 as Jeconiah. While the legal right to the throne passed to Jesus through Joseph, the physical right came through Mary by the line of descendants from Nathan, the son of David.

Christ's birth fulfilled the Old Testament prophecy. He was born of the Virgin Mary (Isa. 7:14; Matt. 1:22–25), and He was born in Bethlehem (Mic. 5:2; Luke 2:4–7). He was the Almighty God, conceived by the Holy Spirit (Isa. 9:6–7; Luke 1:34–38).

The Humanity of Christ

The fact of Christ's genuine humanity is implicit in all of the Old Testament prophecies that describe His lineage, His life on earth, and His resurrection. The New Testament accounts confirm this by reporting that Mary was His virgin mother and that He went through the normal processes of gestation, birth, childhood, and development into manhood. There is no intimation that anyone ever questioned His humanity during His life on earth; only after His ascension into heaven did pagan philosophic theories begin to suggest otherwise.

The New Testament states explicitly: "And the Word became flesh" (John 1:14; see also Heb. 2:14). He had a body (Heb. 10:5), as confirmed in all the Gospel narratives, a human soul (Matt. 26:38; Mark 14:34), and a spirit (Matt. 27:50). The doctrine of the humanity of Christ is absolutely essential to the Christian faith, for without His genuine humanity, He would not have had a genuine death on the cross and could not have fulfilled His work as prophet, priest, and king.

The Deity of Christ

Both the Old and New Testaments bear abundant testimony to the deity of Christ, and all denials of His deity
involve denying scriptural revelation. According to Isaiah
9:6–7 Christ is the "Mighty God" who, according to Isaiah
7:14, would be called Immanuel, meaning God with us.
The opening verses of John's gospel also affirm that Jesus
Christ was the Word, or revelation, of God, and that He is
eternal and all that God is: "In the beginning was the
Word, and the Word was with God, and the Word was God.
He was in the beginning with God" (John 1:1–2). As God,
Christ was the creator: "All things were made through
Him, and without Him nothing was made that was made"
(John 1:3). This is confirmed in Colossians 1:16, "For by
Him all things were created that are in heaven and that
are on earth, visible and invisible, whether thrones or
dominions or principalities or powers. All things were
created through Him and for Him." The fact that He is
also eternal is confirmed in Colossians 1:17: "And He is
before all things, and in Him all things consist." He is not
only the creator, but the sustainer of the universe.

His deity is further attested to by the divine name
assigned Him, including the word *Jehovah* or *Yahweh*,
and the attributes of God ascribed to Him in both the Old
and New Testaments. His immutability, or changeless-
ness, is described in Hebrews 13:8: "Jesus Christ is the
same yesterday, today, and forever" (see also Heb. 1:10–
12). He is omnipotent, as stated in Revelation 1:8: " 'I am
the Alpha and the Omega, the Beginning and the End,'
says the Lord, 'who is and who was and who is to come,
the Almighty' " (see also Isa. 9:6; Phil. 3:21). He is omniscient and knows all things: "But Jesus did not commit
Himself to them, because He knew all men, and had no
need that anyone should testify of man, for He knew what
was in man" (John 2:24–25; see also John 21:17; Rev.
2:19). He is omnipresent, as indicated in Matthew 28:20
where Christ said, "And lo, I am with you always, even to
the end of the age" (see also Matt. 18:20; John 1:50 and

3:13). All the attributes of God are in Christ: "For in
Christ all the fullness of the Deity lives in bodily form"
(Col. 2:9 NIV).

His works confirm the fact that He is God. As stated in
Matthew 9:2–7, He can forgive sin. Jesus Himself declared, "the Son of Man has power on earth to forgive sins"
(Matt. 9:6; see also Mark 2:7–10; Col. 3:13). He is the
judge of all men: "For the Father judges no one, but has
committed all judgment to the Son" (John 5:22; see also
Acts 10:42; 17:31; 2 Tim. 4:1). He also has the power to
raise the dead: "Do not marvel at this; for the hour is
coming in which all who are in the graves will hear His
voice and come forth—those who have done good, to the
resurrection of life, and those who have done evil, to the
resurrection of condemnation" (John 5:28–29; see also
Rev. 1:18).

The crowning evidence is His resurrection from the
dead. Accordingly, all prophecy concerning Jesus Christ
is based on His deity as well as His humanity. The
ultimate purpose of prophetic fulfillment is to demonstrate that Jesus Christ is the Son of God, the true King of
kings and Lord of lords.

Christ Held the Office of a Prophet

According to the prophecy in Deuteronomy 18:15, 18–
19, when Jesus came He would be a prophet like Moses.
Verse 15 says, "The LORD your God will raise up for you a
prophet like me from among your own brothers. You must
listen to him" (NIV). Philip pointed out that Jesus was the
one who fulfilled Moses' prophecy, saying, "We have found
the one Moses wrote about in the Law, and about whom
the prophets also wrote—Jesus of Nazareth, the son of
Joseph" (John 1:45 NIV; see also Acts 3:22–23; 7:37).

Christ repeatedly claimed to be speaking the words of
God (John 7:16; 12:49–50; 14:24; 17:8). On one occasion
He said, "My teaching is not my own. It comes from him
who sent me" (John 7:16 NIV).

Christ fulfilled every aspect of prophecy about His ministry. We find the evidence in His major discourses and His

predictions concerning His own death, burial, resurrection, and ascension. Therefore, we know He will also fulfill
the prophecy of His second coming. In addition He made
prophetic pronouncements on almost every important
theological theme relating to the destiny of men and angels, the character and course of the present age, and the
emergence of the church, its history, and its future rapture. He revealed in detail the end-time events of the
great tribulation, the coming of the Antichrist, His own
messianic kingdom, and His judgment of all men in the
eternal state. Not only was Christ a prophet, He was the
most important prophet. He spoke more prophecies than
any other prophet in Scripture.

Christ Is a Priest

Both the Melchizedek and Aaronic priesthoods predicted
the office and function of Christ's priesthood. Like Aaron,
He was appointed by God: "So also Christ did not glorify
Himself to become High Priest, but it was He who said to
Him: 'You are My Son, today I have begotten You' " (Heb.
5:5).

Like Melchizedek the incarnate Christ was a genuine
man (Heb. 2:14; 1 Tim. 2:5) and the king (Gen. 14:18; Zech.
6:13). Unlike the Aaronic priesthood, Melchizedek has no
recorded lineage leading to Christ, and Christ's priesthood
was not based on a human inheritance. Hebrews 7:3
states, "Without father, without mother, without geneal-
ogy, having neither beginning of days nor end of life, but
made like the Son of God, remains a priest forever." As
Melchizedek was never succeeded by another, so Christ
will not have a successor. He will continue forever. Because of this, Hebrews 7:25 states, "Therefore He is also
able to save to the uttermost those who come to God
through Him, since He always lives to make intercession
for them." The prophecy in Psalm 110:4 confirms this:

> The LORD has sworn
> And will not relent,
> "You are a priest forever
> According to the order of Melchizedek."

The sacrificial system of the Old Testament, both in its patriarchal form before the law of Moses and its Aaronic form under the law of Moses, foreshadowed the work of Christ as a priest. In His life and death Christ fulfilled the three basic functions of a priest: sacrifice, intercession, and giving gifts. As our high priest, Christ gave Himself as a sacrifice, engages in intercession for us, and bestows upon us many spiritual blessings (Heb. 7:25). In contrast to the Old Testament priests who had to offer many sacrifices and whose intercession ceased at retirement or death, Christ offered one sacrifice for sin and now intercedes forever on the basis of it (John 17:1–26; Rom. 8:34; Heb. 7:25; 9:24). In the present age, believers belong to the royal priesthood and offer up spiritual sacrifices and intercession through Christ, their high priest (Heb. 13:15 – 16; 1 Peter 2:5).

Christ Is King

From a prophetic standpoint, the most important office of Christ is that of being King of kings and Lord of lords. God promised David a descendant who would sit on his throne forever (2 Sam. 7:1–17). Many passages in the Old Testament anticipate the coming of Christ as King and His reign over the earth on David's throne (Ps. 89:35–36; Isa. 9:6–7; Jer. 23:5–8; see chapter 6).

The angel's announcement to Mary in Luke 1:31 – 33 confirms the prediction that Christ will set up His throne on earth at His second coming (Matt. 25:31) and Peter's prediction that Christ will reign on the throne of David (Acts 2:29 – 31). Paul refers to this in 1 Corinthians 15:24 – 28, and Revelation 20:4–6 anticipates that Christ will reign on earth for one thousand years.

Interpreted literally, these prophecies predict that at His second coming Christ will set up a kingdom on earth to fulfill the Davidic promise and will reign on earth for one thousand years before the new heaven and the new earth replace our present earth. Christ will not only rule over Israel, but He will rule over the entire earth as King of kings and Lord of lords (Ps. 72:8–11; Isa. 2:1–4:11; Jer.

23:5–8; Dan. 7:14; Matt. 25:31–46; Rev. 19:15–16).

The Life of Christ on Earth

Christ's life on earth fulfilled hundreds of Old Testament prophecies, including those concerning His conception, birth in Bethlehem, and His preaching and healing ministry. Christ referred to this in reading Isaiah 61:1–2 in the synagogue at Nazareth. Christ's first coming partially fulfilled this passage, which also refers to His second advent (Luke 4:21). Fulfilled in Christ's first advent was the prediction of a prophetic ministry of preaching good tidings, a healing ministry of aiding those broken in body and mind, and His work as the Savior in giving liberty to captives. Some passages, such as Isaiah 35, which refer primarily to the future millennial kingdom, anticipated Christ would heal the blind and the deaf and cause the lame to leap for joy (Isa. 35:5–6). These fulfilled prophecies form an important confirmation of the truth and accuracy of prophecy.

The Death of Christ

The death of Christ on the cross, anticipated by the sacrificial offerings of the Old Testament, fulfilled in detail such prophecies as those found in Psalm 22 and Isaiah 53 (see also Gen. 3:15; Isa. 50:6; Zech. 12:10; 13:6–7). The sufferings of Christ predicted in the Old Testament are a major theme connecting it and the New Testament.

In His death, Christ also fulfilled His own predictions concerning His death (Matt. 16:21; 17:22–23; 20:17–19; 26:12, 28, 31; Mark 9:32–34; 14:8, 24, 27; Luke 9:22, 44–45; 18:31–34; 22:20; John 2:19–21; 10:17–18; 12:7). Many other references, such as John 3:14; 6:51; 10:11; 11:49–52; 12:24; 15:13, anticipate the death of Christ indirectly. The death of Christ is a major prophetic theme of both the Old and New Testaments.

The Resurrection of Christ

Every reference to Christ's works after His death clearly anticipates His resurrection. Psalm 16:9–10 affirms that Christ would not remain in the tomb and His body would never decay (i.e., "corruption"). Quoted by Peter in Acts 2:24–31 and again by Paul in Acts 13:34–37, this Old Testament passage clearly predicts Christ's resurrection. Psalm 22:22 and 118:22–24 refer to Christ's role following His resurrection. Christ, as a fulfillment of the Melchizedek-type priest, would also continue as a priest forever (Gen. 14:18; Heb. 7:15–17, 23–25).

It was absolutely necessary for Christ to rise from the dead, not only to affirm His deity, but also to fulfill His continuing role as priest and king. Christ frequently predicted His own resurrection, and it literally fulfilled these prophecies, which form a central doctrine for the Christian faith.

The Second Coming

Prophecies of Christ's second coming are a major theme in both the Old and New Testaments, and all major orthodox creeds of the Church include this doctrine. Important passages in the Old Testament that predict the Second Coming include Deuteronomy 30:3; Psalm 2:1 – 9; 24:1 – 10; 50:1 – 5; 96:10 – 13; 110:1; Isaiah 9:7; 11:10 – 12; 63:1 – 6; Jeremiah 23:5 – 6; Ezekiel 37:21 – 22; Daniel 2:44 – 45; 7:13 – 14; Hosea 3:4 – 5; Micah 4:7; Zechariah 2:10 – 12; 6:12 – 13; 12:10; 13:1 – 9; 14:3 – 4.

The Second Coming is also found in many passages in the New Testament (Matt. 19:28; 23:39; 24:27 – 31; 25:6, 31 – 46; Luke 12:35 – 40; 17:24 – 36; 18:8; 21:25 – 28; 24:25 – 26; Acts 1:10 – 11; 15:16 – 18; Rom. 11:25 – 26; 2 Thess. 2:8; 1 Tim. 6:14 – 15; James 5:7 – 8; 2 Peter 3:3 – 4; Jude 1:14 – 15; Rev. 1:7 – 8; 2:25 – 28; 16:15; 19:11 – 21; 20:4 – 6; 22:20). According to these Scriptures, Christ will return bodily to the earth with great power and glory, just as He ascended in the clouds into heaven (Rev. 19:11 – 21).

When Christ returns, He will assume the throne of His father David (Luke 1:32 – 33; Acts 2:19 – 20; Rev. 20:4 – 6). He will subdue the earth with His mighty power (Rev. 19:11–21), judge both Israel and the nations (Ezek. 20:34–

38; Matt. 25:31–46), and bring blessing and renewal to the earth (Isa. 35). No one can claim that these prophecies have been fulfilled in history; they will be fulfilled only by Christ's second coming.

In addition to prophecies concerning the Second Coming, the New Testament also reveals promises about the rapture and Christ's coming for the church. Many interpreters believe these events will precede the end-time events and will occur before the Second Coming (1 Cor. 15:51–58; 1 Thess. 4:13–18; see chapter 9).

Taken as a whole, prophecies relating to Jesus Christ are a major theme of the Old and New Testaments and are an integral part of the Christian faith. (For further discussion see chapter 11.) Because many prophecies have been accurately, completely, and literally fulfilled, we know the rest will be fulfilled also. This knowledge leads to a better understanding of those events that have been predicted but have not yet occurred.

3

THE THIRD KEY
The Covenants

Scripture abounds in predictions about the future that reveal God's promises. Some of these concern particular events or things God Himself will do. Some predict the actions of men or of creatures. And some are comprehensive covenants in which God declares His purpose to fulfill certain objectives.

The Theological Covenants

The systematic statement of God's broad purposes in the universe described in theology includes at least two major covenants: the covenant of grace and the covenant of redemption. These actually refer to the same act in which God provided grace and redemption through the sacrifice of Christ.

God's purpose in providing us grace and redemption is often referred to as *predestination*. In Romans 8:29–30 Paul states, "For whom He foreknew, He also predestined to be conformed to the image of His Son, that He might be the firstborn among many brethren. Moreover whom He predestined, these He also called; whom He called, these He also justified; and whom He justified, these He also glorified." Verses 4, 5, and 11 of Ephesians 1 state a similar truth: "He chose us in Him before the foundation of the world, that we should be holy and without blame before Him in love, having predestined us to adoption as sons by Jesus Christ to Himself, according to the good pleasure of His will. . . . In Him also we have obtained an inheritance, being predestined according to the purpose of Him who works all things according to the counsel of His will." Though students of Scripture often have difficulty comprehending exactly what predestination means, clearly it is a biblical doctrine.

Other passages, such as Romans 9:11 and Ephesians 3:11, reveal predestination as God's purpose in eternity past. First Peter 1:20 refers to Christ as the Redeemer "chosen before the creation of the world" (NIV). Other passages declare "this grace was given us in Christ Jesus before the beginning of time" (2 Tim. 1:9 NIV) and that eternal life was "promised before the beginning of time" (Titus 1:2 NIV).

Because God is omniscient, when He determined in advance that some would be saved, He knew all the possibilities of any plan He would adopt. In predestination, as in all of God's eternal purposes, He determined not only how He would provide salvation, but also how men would respond under different circumstances. The plan God chose does not force anyone to be saved or lost, but means simply that He knows in advance what each of us will do. While this concept is difficult for us to comprehend with our limited understanding of infinite truth, if there had been a better, more feasible plan, we can be assured that God would have undertaken it. By giving mankind the ability to make choices, He allows some to make bad choices and others to make good ones. Overall, there is, however, the providential work of God to accomplish His will, and Christians can rejoice in the fact that we are included in God's plan.

These references make clear that God's decision to save believers was not an afterthought or a change in plans when sin entered the universe. Rather, it was a part of His eternal plan put in place before creation ever began.

Students of theology raise the question of why God chose to create and begin human history when it would cost Him the death of His Son. He did this to reveal His infinite perfection. In creation He demonstrates His omnipotence, omniscience, and sovereignty. Only in redemption, however, could God reveal His love, His righteousness, and His grace. Accordingly, human history, with all its details, is related to God's revealing who He is. In creating the angels, some of whom sinned, were immediately judged, and thrown out of heaven to become Satan and his demons, God displayed His righteousness. With mankind, however, He not only displayed His righteousness, but His love by providing salvation through the death of Jesus Christ. The theological covenants undergird all of the Scriptures and reveal God's sovereign purpose.

The Biblical Covenants

In addition to God's eternal promise of salvation, the Scriptures also reveal certain promises that will be fulfilled in human time as well as in eternity. The truth about God and His ways is not all revealed at once. It begins in the Garden of Eden, unfolds throughout the Old Testament, and climaxes in the New Testament. We find a series of biblical covenants largely concerning God's moral revelation and His purpose for and requirements of mankind. This is indicated by the fact that our Bible is divided into the Old and New Testaments, or the Old Covenant and the New Covenant. With the term "Old Covenant," we refer to all the covenants described in the Old Testament. "New Covenant" refers to the new Covenant of Grace established by the birth, death, and resurrection of Jesus Christ. John summarizes this succinctly in John 1:17: "For the law was given through Moses, but grace and truth came through Jesus Christ."

In the Law of Moses, which permeates all of the Old Testament except the book of Genesis, God set forth a rule of life for Israel which included important promises of both blessing and judgment. When we speak of the Old Covenant we are referring to these promises. However, when God made the Old Covenant with Israel, there were already other covenants that had also governed the behavior and responsibility of mankind until that time. Therefore, those previous promises became a part of the Old Covenant. In addition, God used the Old Covenant to introduce a new covenant that would come later, and He introduced it with prophecy.

The Rule of Innocence

In the creation of Adam and Eve, God charged them with the simple responsibility of taking charge of His physical creation. His purpose was to "let them have dominion over the fish of the sea, over the birds of the air, and over the cattle, over all the earth and over every creeping thing that creeps on the earth" (Gen. 1:26). God commanded them, "Be fruitful and multiply; fill the earth and subdue it; have dominion over the fish of the sea, over the birds of the air, and over every living thing that moves on the earth" (v. 28). He offered them the food provided by the plant life on the earth, but He did not authorize man to eat meat (vv. 29–30). The only command He gave them that had important moral significance regarded the tree of the knowledge of good and evil. He told them, "Of every tree of the garden you may freely eat; but of the tree of the knowledge of good and evil you shall not eat, for in the day that you eat of it you shall surely die" (2:16–17). It was this relatively simple prohibition that caused the Fall and allowed sin to enter the world. Eve and then Adam disobeyed God and ate the fruit of this tree.

The Rule of Conscience

After Adam and Eve fell into sin, God gave them consciences, the ability to distinguish between right and wrong. The record of this rule of life begins in Genesis 3:7 and ends in 8:19. The details of the responsibilities of Adam and Eve are not extensive. They were required to live according to their consciences and in keeping with the knowledge of good and evil God had given them.

While mankind now had the ability to distinguish good from evil and the individual's conscience could convict him of his sin, the conscience had no power in itself to produce moral perfection. The New Testament emphasizes this point in many passages and in many ways (see, for example, John 8:7–9; 1 Cor. 8:7; and 1 Tim. 4:1–2). Paul records his own struggle with his conscience in Romans 7, pointing out in verse 21 and following that while he wanted to serve the Lord completely, instead he did evil. The fact is the conscience, even though active in a Christian, does not in itself create the ability to conquer a sinful nature. Only through Christ can one be victorious over sin. Paul put it succinctly when he said, "O wretched man that I am! Who will deliver me from this body of death? I thank God—through Jesus Christ our Lord!" (vv. 24–25).

When sin entered the world, man received a sinful nature. From this point the history of mankind demonstrates a rejection of God's revelation and morality. Cain profoundly illustrated this when he rejected God's instructions about the sacrifice of an animal (Gen. 4:5) and, in the resulting dispute with Abel, killed his brother (v. 8). The history of mankind from that point on is one of increasing wickedness, resulting ultimately in God's severe judgment (6:5, 11–13). Cain faced individual judgment (4:10–15) and through him physical death overtook man (Gen. 5). Eventually, man's sinful nature resulted in the destruction of civilization, except for Noah and his family, by an all encompassing flood (7:21–24).

God's judgments, however, did not diminish the fact that He can and does extend divine grace. He extended grace to Noah who, although a righteous man, was not perfect (6:8–10; Heb. 11:7), and to Enoch by sparing him physical death (Gen. 5:24). As a whole, the rule of conscience acknowledged that man, knowing the difference between good and evil, would not necessarily choose good. In this period, as in all other periods of human history, God revealed His grace to some, His sovereignty to others, and His ability to judge sin to all.

The Rule of Human Government

Beginning with Noah, God introduced a new principle—human government. While Scripture does not mention details of this, Noah received a special covenant that extended to the human race from that point on (Gen. 8:20 – 11:9). Inherent in this covenant was the promise that never again would there be total destruction by flood. Many of the laws of nature would continue unchanged, such as that of the seasons (8:22), and God repeated some of the commands originally given in the Garden of Eden, for example, the one to multiply (9:1); and God gave Noah the responsibility to rule over the animal world (9:2). Through God's covenant with Noah, for the first time mankind could eat the flesh of animals, although consuming their blood was still forbidden (v. 4). The most important aspect of the rule of human government, however, was God's new commandment to kill those who murdered others (vv. 5–6). This, of course, is the essence of human government and another factor in controlling the morality of mankind.

The scriptural record shows that this rule of life failed to produce holiness just as the previous ones had failed. This is indicated in Noah's drunkenness (9:21), Ham's ridiculing Noah, his father (v. 22), and, in general, mankind's deterioration and departure from God (11:1–4). This period climaxed in the Tower of Babel, when man's ability to speak one language was confounded and consequently human civilization was scattered (11:4–9). This rule of life, however, like the previous ones, reveals evidence of God's grace, and out of it came a new order that God introduced to Abraham.

The Rule of Promise

Although different rules of life supplanted each other, some continue to affect human history. Innocence ended in the Garden of Eden, but conscience and human government continued ultimately in complicated forms. The promise given to Abraham and the covenant with him will continue into eternity.

As a specific covenant with Abraham, however, the rule of promise was central in God's dealings with the human race as revealed from Genesis 11:10 to Exodus 19:2, when the Law of Moses was introduced.

As detailed in Genesis 12:2–3; 13:6; 15:5, 18–21; 17:7–8; 28:13–14; and Joshua 1:2–4, God stated the broad promises He would fulfill through Abraham. Abraham was to be a great man (Gen. 12:1–2). God promised him a great nation, fulfilled primarily in Israel, though other nations descended from him, as well (Gen. 12:2; 16:15; 25:2). But most important was the promise of blessing given to the entire world (12:3). These promises of the Abrahamic Covenant are already almost completely fulfilled. We recognize Abraham today as an important prophet of the Old Testament and a vehicle of God's divine revelation. From Abraham descended Isaac, Jacob, and the twelve sons of Jacob who led the twelve tribes of Israel. Others also descended from Abraham by way of Ishmael, Esau, and the sons of Keturah (25:2). The Arab world, at least in part, is descended from Abraham.

Abraham is mentioned many times in Scripture and revered by Judaism and the Muslim faith as well. Obviously, God's promise to Abraham of many descendants has been fulfilled. But, most importantly, the promise of blessing to the entire world was fulfilled preeminently in Christ and in the writing of the Scriptures, largely by Jewish pens. God has seen fit to reveal Himself to the entire world through Israel, and the present church, largely Gentile, owes its origin to people of Jewish faith.

The fulfillment of the promises of the Abrahamic Covenant are absolutely sure and unconditional. Some aspects of the covenant, however, were conditional as far as any one generation was concerned, and the blessings of the covenant extended primarily to those of faith.

One of the most important promises concerned the land. It is mentioned in Genesis 12:7: "To your descendants I will give this land." The concept of God's giving the land to Abraham's descendants has become a watershed in the study of prophecy. The tendency has been to deny this is a literal promise. Study reveals, however, that throughout the Old Testament the land is always literally the land described in Genesis 15:15–18—the area from the river of Egypt to the River Euphrates. Prophecy specifies that Israel will be regathered to this land and installed in this land in connection with Christ's second coming. The present movement of Israel back to the land and their formation of a political state seem to be the beginning of the fulfillment of this promise. For these reasons the covenant with Abraham is described as absolutely sure and everlasting (Gen. 17:7, 13, 19; 1 Chron. 16:16–17; Ps. 105:10). The fact that it is everlasting is in itself a declaration that the covenant will certainly be fulfilled.

Unfortunately, there was failure under the rule of promise, just as there had been failure in previous periods. When Abraham was given the original promise about the land, he was to go to it and possess it, but he delayed. Accompanied by his father and Lot, and contrary to God's instructions, Abraham remained in Haran until his father died (Gen. 11:31–32). Then Abraham proceeded to the Promised Land and began the initial possession.

The delayed birth of Isaac also tested Abraham's faith that God would keep the covenant and resulted in Abraham's committing another act of unbelief: his siring Ishmael. Not until Abraham was one hundred years old, many years after he received the promise, did he father Isaac (Gen. 21:1–3). The birth was a supernatural miracle, because both Abraham and Sarah were beyond childbearing age (Gen. 17:15–19; 18:13–14; 21:4–7).

Although Abraham became a man of supreme faith and was willing to offer Isaac as a sacrifice (Gen. 22), there was much failure in his life. The idea that Abraham and other men of old were unusual saints has to be qualified by the evidence. Contrary to God's direction, Abraham went down to Egypt (Gen. 12:10–13:1), which was a lapse of faith about God's capacity to care for his family in the land. Following Abraham's compromise, Isaac lived near Egypt, although he did not go there as he had hoped he would (Gen. 26:6–16). Jacob, the son of Isaac, relied on deceit to obtain for himself his older brother's birthright. Eventually, Abraham's descendants followed Jacob into Egypt where they remained for hundreds of years. Their spiritual defection while in Egypt is all too evident (Ex. 2:23; 4:1–10; 5:21; 14:10–12; 15:24).

Once the Israelites started out for the Promised Land, they encountered problems, wanted to go back (Gen. 14:10 – 12), and constantly complained about God's dealings with them (Ex. 15:24; 16:2; Num. 14:2; 16:11, 41; Joshua 9:18). This led to their act of unbelief at Kadesh-Barnea (Num. 14), which resulted in their wandering in the wilderness for forty years. It is significant, however, that although they failed and there was delay in possessing the land, ultimately the promise was literally fulfilled. Under Joshua the people of Israel occupied a portion of the Promised Land. From these events we can understand that the covenant continues today and extends into eternity.

The Rule of Mosaic Law

Most of the Old Testament from Exodus forward deals with God's revelation of His moral and religious commands to Moses and succeeding generations. The first five books of the Old Testament were written during Moses' lifetime and are a major compilation of religious and moral law.

The Law falls into three divisions. First, the commandments (Ex. 20:1–26), which reveal God's will in certain moral issues; second, His judgments relating to the social-civil life of Israel (Ex. 21:1–24:11); and finally the religious ordinances He wanted the people to keep (Ex. 24:12–31:18). These regulations (more than six hundred) were the foundation for Israel's moral relationship with God.

There is no evidence that God ever required those who were not of the nation Israel to observe these laws. Therefore, the Mosaic Covenant was with the people of Israel only. Essentially it went a step beyond human government and created a theocracy in which prophets, priests, and later kings governed the nation. Unlike the rule of conscience, the rule of human government, and the cove-

nant with Abraham, the Bible says that Mosaic Law ended
with the death of Christ (Gal. 3:24–25).

Mosaic Law provided many conditions for blessings
related to earthly life and states the rules of forgiveness,
sacrifice, and how man can live in harmony with God.
Unlike the preceding rules of life, the blessings of Mosaic
Law were conditional. The Law did not give eternal promises and did not provide a way of salvation. Eternal life in
heaven was not one of its rewards, nor hell one of its
judgments. The Law related only to this life and God's
rule over the people of Israel.

As the New Testament makes clear, Mosaic Law did not
bring holiness to the Israelites. Instead, their pattern of
failure exceeded anything that had happened before. The
fact of knowing God's will does not necessarily empower
His people to obey it. Many generations of Israel completely forgot the Law. They neglected their need to offer
sacrifices and eventually stopped offering them. Even the
priests departed from the faith and began worshiping
idols. This disobedience resulted in a series of severe
judgments, including the Babylonian and Assyrian captivities when the people of Israel were taken away from the
Promised Land, and ultimately, after Jewish leaders rejected Christ, were scattered all over the world following
the destruction of Jerusalem in A.D. 70.

These rules of life in effect prior to the coming of Christ
make clear that once sin entered the human race, man was
inherently incapable of making the moral choices that
would honor God and correspond to His holy standards.
Exceptions to this are the demonstrations of God's grace
and the divine enablement God granted to believers in the
Old Testament and especially in the New Testament.

Although under the Law the emphasis was on righteousness and judgment, grace was manifested in forgiveness when the people met its conditions of sacrifice and
confession. The fact that God was patient often allowed
Israel to depart from His will for generations before judgment finally overtook them. Whenever there was genuine

repentance, God always accepted it. It is significant that even under the Law there is grace. In other words, believers received unmerited favor with God and undeserved forgiveness. Still, Christ needed to come and die in order to provide a righteous basis for God's forgiveness. Romans 3:25–26 tells of the necessity of Christ's sacrifice to justify forgiveness under the Law: "Whom God set forth to be a propitiation by His blood, through faith, to demonstrate His righteousness, because in His forbearance God had passed over the sins that were previously committed, to demonstrate at the present time His righteousness, that He might be just and the justifier of the one who has faith in Jesus."

It is important to note that God never intended Mosaic Law to be a universal rule for all nations. The Law was only for the people of Israel, and failing to keep it resulted in their being judged. We must also remember that the Law did not provide the people with the strength to obey it. It had no power to provide justification (Rom. 3:20; Gal. 2:16). It was not a permanent or unconditional covenant. It would be in effect for only a limited time (Gen. 3:19). The Law did not promise new birth (Gal. 3:21–22). It only provided a way to identify sin and departure from God. It proved that without divine grace mankind could not be saved or restored to and reconciled with God (Rom. 3:19).

All of this pointed to Christ and reaffirmed the need for a new rule, one of grace. None of the rules of life in the Old Testament had salvation as their major purpose, but consisted of rules of morality in keeping with God's will. In all these periods, salvation could be only by grace and, ultimately, would have to be based on the death of Christ.

The Rule of Grace

John 1:17 summarizes the new rule of grace: "The law was given through Moses, but grace and truth came through Jesus Christ." The New Testament is a fuller revelation of God, His grace, the way of salvation, and His plans for believers. The present age of the rule of grace contrasts with the Mosaic period when Mosaic Law ruled

supreme over Israel. Mosaic Law ruled by regulation. But
grace, while it has its moral standards, is not a merit
system wherein rewards depend on good works. The New
Covenant, promised from creation and set in place by
Christ's death and resurrection, reveals that God gra-
ciously forgives, cares for, and sustains believers even if
they do not deserve it.

The new rule of grace was predicted in the Old Testament with the terminology "a new covenant." Jeremiah
prophesied that a new covenant would supplant the Mosaic Covenant when he said:

> Behold, the days are coming, says the LORD, when I will
> make a new covenant with the house of Israel and with the
> house of Judah—not according to the covenant that I made
> with their fathers in the day that I took them by the hand
> to lead them out of the land of Egypt, My covenant which
> they broke, though I was a husband to them, says the
> LORD.
>
> But this is the covenant that I will make with the house
> of Israel: After those days, says the LORD: I will put My
> law in their minds, and write it on their hearts; and I will
> be their God, and they shall be My people. No more shall
> every man teach his neighbor, and every man his brother,
> saying, "Know the LORD," for they all shall know Me, from
> the least of them to the greatest of them, says the LORD.
> For I will forgive their iniquity, and their sin I will remem-
> ber no more.   (Jer. 31:31–34; see also Ezek. 37:21–28)

In the New Covenant, God would be gracious to the
people of Israel. He would forgive them, plant His Law in
their hearts, and be their God, and He would forgive their
wickedness and remember their sins no more. This prophecy was fulfilled and the New Covenant was made possible
when Jesus Christ came into the world, died on a cross for
the sins of the world, and rose again. Through His death
and resurrection, God released grace—undeserved favor
and undeserved forgiveness—to those who would trust
Him. Just as Jeremiah prophesied, the New Covenant
replaced the Mosaic Covenant.

Those who believe Christ will inaugurate a millennial

earthly kingdom believe the New Covenant for Israel will be fulfilled primarily at the time of the Second Coming. It is obvious, however, that when Christ came initially, He introduced a new covenant that is not only for Israel but relates to the Church also (Luke 22:20; 1 Cor. 11:25; 2 Cor. 3:6; Heb. 8:8; 9:15).

Scholars differ on how to explain this. Probably the best explanation is that the death of Christ introduced a new covenant of grace into God's dealings with all mankind. As this covenant applies to Israel, it will be fulfilled in the future. As it applies to the present age, however, it is being fulfilled in the Church. The elements of the Lord's Supper are symbolic of the new covenant of grace that the Church enjoys. Actually, salvation, which is an integral part of the New Covenant, is found all through the Bible; everyone who is saved, from Adam to the last person in the future who enters salvation, finds salvation on the basis of the New Covenant that Christ brought into being by His death on the cross.

In initiating the Lord's Supper, the night before His crucifixion, Christ said to His disciples, "This cup is the new covenant in My blood, which is shed for you" (Luke 22:20). This is the application of the New Covenant to the Church, the believers of the present age.

At the heart of the present rule of grace is the revelation of the God who transforms a believer from condemnation in Adam to justification in Christ. The rule of grace assures that when a person has been regenerated by faith in Christ, he has been born again. Titus 3:5 states: "Not by works of righteousness which we have done, but according to His mercy He saved us, through the washing of regeneration and renewing of the Holy Spirit." We can assume that all people who are saved in every age are born again at the time of their salvation, but the Old Testament is not nearly as clear as the New Testament on this point. In His conversation with Nicodemus, Jesus plainly said that new birth is essential to salvation: "Most assuredly, I say to you, unless one is born of water and the Spirit, he cannot enter the kingdom of God. That which is born of the flesh is flesh, and that which is born of the Spirit is spirit. Do not marvel that I said to you, 'You must be born again' " (John 3:5–7).

Occurring simultaneously with new birth in the present age is baptism by the Holy Spirit. This was initiated on the Day of Pentecost but is now fulfilled for every believer at the moment of salvation. According to 1 Corinthians 12:13, "For by one Spirit we were all baptized into one body—whether Jews or Greeks, whether slaves or free— and have all been made to drink into one Spirit." The baptism of the Holy Spirit sets believers of the present age apart from those who were saved before the present age began, as well as setting aside those who will be saved after the rapture of the church. The baptism forms both Jew and Gentile, regardless of race, into the one living organism that is described as the Church of Jesus Christ.

Another tremendous change brought about by the New Covenant is that every believer in the present age, in contrast to believers of Old Testament times, is constantly indwelt by the Holy Spirit. Paul reminded the Corinthians of this when he wrote them saying, "Do you not know that your body is the temple of the Holy Spirit who is in you, whom you have from God, and you are not your own?" (1 Cor. 6:19). Because the Holy Spirit indwells us, He Himself is our seal, or token of security, until we are resurrected: "In Him you also trusted, after you heard the word of truth, the gospel of your salvation; in whom also, having believed, you were sealed with the Holy Spirit of promise, who is the guarantee of our inheritance until the redemption of the purchased possession, to the praise of His glory" (Eph. 1:13–14). Never before in the history of the world had believers enjoyed the distinctives of regeneration, baptism, indwelling, and sealing of the Holy Spirit. But that is not all.

Under the new covenant any believer can be filled with the Spirit. Paul said, "Do not be drunk with wine, in which is dissipation; but be filled with the Spirit" (Eph. 5:18). In the Old Testament an individual was filled by the Spirit largely as God's sovereign work to prepare him for a particular task. After Christ's death, however, any believer who yields his life to God and who allows it can be filled by the Spirit.

In addition to these rich provisions as a basis for our spiritual lives, the New Testament reveals much more than the Old about God, His grace, His love, His wisdom, His righteousness, and His plans for believers in Christ in the present age, as well as in the future. Among the precious truths added by the New Covenant is the doctrine of the rapture of the church. It provides for Christ to come ultimately to remove believers from the world and take them to heaven before the final judgments of the Great Tribulation take place.

The present rule of grace characterizes what the New Testament calls the Church, the body of true believers knit together by the baptism of the Spirit, who enjoy regeneration and are related to Christ as a living body is related to its head. Grace and truth do indeed come by Jesus Christ, and they come in abundant measure.

The Rule of the Future Kingdom

Those who believe Christ will introduce a thousand-year kingdom after His second coming also expect the kingdom to endure and continue to rule after the thousand years has ended. This comprehensive doctrine is discussed at length in the Old Testament. For Israel, the new kingdom will fulfill the promises of the New Covenant. When Christ returns, in a series of judgments He will wipe out all adults who are unsaved, resurrect the righteous who have not been previously raised from the dead, and rule as King of kings on the throne of David in the capital city of Jerusalem.

"Come, and let us go up to the mountain of the LORD,
To the house of the God of Jacob;
He will teach us His ways,
And we shall walk in His paths."
For out of Zion shall go forth the law,
And the word of the LORD from Jerusalem.

> He shall judge between the nations,
> And rebuke many people.   (Isa. 2:3–4)

The millennial kingdom will be both a spiritual and a political kingdom, with Christ reigning as King of kings and Lord of lords. More details of this aspect of divine revelation will be considered in chapter 12.

The Rules of Life as Dispensations

The word *dispensation* embodies Scripture's rules of life. A dispensation is a divinely revealed system of morals, values, promises, and rules that God imposes on a particular generation. In that sense, each of the rules of life of the Old Testament is a dispensation. For centuries, systematic theologians have referred to these stewardships as dispensations, or periods, in which God tested man with particular circumstances. In the Garden of Eden, for example, God tested mankind with the dispensation of innocence, followed by the dispensation of conscience, and so on through history.

Various systems of dispensation can be found throughout the history of the Church. Whether they use the actual word or not, all theologians recognize God's progressive revelation that added requirements for man's government in successive ages. In some cases, new revelation superseded previous revelation and changed the requirements. Although God's morality and the Bible's basic value systems do not change, nevertheless, in the present age of the Church no one attempts to follow many of the detailed instructions included in the Law of Moses.

The Christian church sets aside Sunday, the day of the resurrection, for the sabbath, rather than Saturday, the last day of the week designated as the sabbath in Old Testament times. God instructed Moses to kill a person who broke the Sabbath day by gathering sticks (Num. 15:32–36). Today we would consider that murder, but under the Law the penalty was just. Many of the hundreds of requirements specified by the Law of Moses, such as offering animal sacrifices and going to Jerusalem for the feasts, are not observed today. The present dispensation is different.

Unfortunately in modern times the doctrine of dispensations has been at the center of controversy. C.I. Scofield taught a popular system of dispensations in which he recognized seven dispensations as rules of life. This system came from his belief in the premillennial return of Christ and the millennial kingdom following the Second Coming. Both are basic beliefs of conservative Christianity and, consequently, liberal theologians identified the subject of dispensations with conservative theology. It became their object of attack in the liberal/conservative controversies of the twentieth century.

The controversies became particularly evident in the 1930s when, for the first time, pastors who were graduates of liberal seminaries began to assume leadership roles in churches that formerly were conservative. They soon discovered that their opposition were largely adherents of Scofield's form of dispensationalism. Although the liberals could not attack the conservatives' basic theology, they did attack the conservatives for being dispensationalists. Because the definition of dispensationalism was vague, attacking it became a method of attacking conservative, or orthodox, theological standards.

The amillennialists—those who denied a literal millennial kingdom—even though they were otherwise conservative in their theology, found they could also attack dispensationalists as a way of refuting premillennial beliefs without getting involved in doctrinal controversies. Ultimately some declared dispensationalism a heresy without its ever being fully defined.

This is a deplorable situation in current theology that has no justifiable historical background. Since the first century the concept that dispensations embrace rules for living has been deeply rooted in Christian theology.

In order to clarify a situation that is very confusing, we must remember there is only one way of salvation—through faith in Jesus Christ. That has been true in every rule and will continue to be true until the last person is saved in the millennial kingdom. Dispensations are not ways to find salvation. They are rules for living for those who are saved on the basis of faith in God. A basic concept of dispensationalism is simply that the rules of life change. The rules of life for the present age are not the same as the rules of life under Moses, nor are they the same as the rules of life will be in the millennial kingdom when Christ will reign from Jerusalem. The dispensational concept of various rules of life, regardless of what it is called, is a basic scriptural concept, and to one degree or another, all theologies that attempt to be biblical recognize it.

Many no longer use the word "dispensation" because they do not want to be involved in controversy. The fact is that rules of life began with Adam and will continue through the kingdom of Christ on earth. Understanding this fact is essential to understanding the Bible and what God demands of believers in every age. Therefore, ignoring dispensational distinctions is wrong. On the other hand, emphasizing dispensationalism and its rules of life beyond the teaching of the Scriptures is also wrong. Salvation and the doctrine of grace as they are found in every age provide both the unity and the diversity of the doctrine of rules of life in Scripture.

4

THE FOURTH KEY

Gentiles

The first eleven chapters of Genesis record broad prophecies concerning the Gentile world. During the period before Abraham's lifetime, prophecy concerned all mankind as one unit until Noah and his three sons lived. The predictions of Genesis 9:24–27 are the first indication that God has differing expectations for various parts of humanity. Noah's three sons and their descendants would have different destinies. Japheth's descendants would become the largest division of the Gentiles. Shem, who would receive God's special blessing, would father a line that eventually would produce the Savior. Ham, the father of Canaan, and his descendants would bear a special curse as God's enemies.

These predictions indicate that humanity would be divided into three major sections descended from Noah's sons. Subsequent history shows at least partial fulfillment of these prophecies. The prophecies that follow concern the nations of the world in relation to the seven great empires.

Egypt

Egypt was the leading nation in the Middle East when the first six books of the Bible were written, and it was in Egypt that Israel grew from a family of seventy to a nation of two or three million. The first scriptural reference to Egypt is in connection with Abraham's visit to that country (Gen. 12:10–13:1), but it became a significant factor in the history of Israel as described in the book of Genesis, beginning with Joseph and continuing until the Abrahamic covenant was partially fulfilled.

Joseph's brothers sold him as a slave, and he was taken to Egypt. Later, during a time of famine, he brought all the family of Jacob to Egypt, where they lived and prospered for several hundred years (Gen. 37:12–36; 46:1–7; 47:10–11).

When Joseph interpreted Pharaoh's dream he prophesied seven years of plenty, followed by seven years of drought. In preparation for the trouble ahead, Pharaoh made Joseph head of the food storage that sustained Egypt (and Israel) in the time of famine that followed (Gen. 41:14 – 43).

In the latter years of Israel's sojourn in Egypt, the ruling monarchy turned against the Israelites and made them slaves. But God's plan was for the nation of Israel to leave Egypt and occupy the Promised Land (Ex. 1:8–14; 12:31–39). Because the Egyptians tried to thwart God's desires for Israel, great judgments fell on Egypt in the form of plagues (Ex. 7–12). The final plague—the death of the firstborn male of both man and beast—caused the Egyptians to be willing to release the Israelites.

Egypt continued to have contact with Israel. Sometimes Egypt was Israel's oppressor and sometimes she acted in other roles. We find major prophecies concerning Egypt in Isaiah 18:1–20:6, which mention that Egypt will be conquered. Some of the references are to the future millennium and some concern events that have occurred and are part of known history. Principal among them is the prophecy that Assyria would conquer Egypt in the days of Assyria's ascendancy. The prophecy was fulfilled with Assyria's invasion beginning about 700 B.C. Isaiah 20:1–6 is a particularly graphic picture of Assyria's domination of Egypt: At God's command, Isaiah went about stripped and barefoot (Isa. 20:3) as a sign of what was going to happen to Egypt when Assyria led off her captives (v. 4).

The point of this prophecy was that Israel should not rely on Egypt for protection. As a nation, Egypt's future was grim, partly because she had oppressed Israel. Under the Abrahamic Covenant, God had promised He would curse the nations that cursed Israel (Gen. 12:3). Babylon would also conquer Egypt, but before this occurred, Egypt would conquer a portion of Israel. King Josiah foolishly went out to attack the Egyptian army (2 Chron. 35:20 – 25) and died in the battle. The people of Israel appointed Jehoahaz as king (2 Chron. 36:1); however, the king of Egypt deposed him and placed Eliakim on the throne in his place (2 Chron. 36:4). The Egyptians' victory was short lived—Babylon soon conquered Israel as well as Egypt, and Babylon and Egypt went down together (2 Chron. 36:6 – 10).

Jeremiah warned Israel not to go down to Egypt, but instead to surrender to the king of Babylon (Jer. 42:7–21). He predicted that if the Israelites did not obey they would "die by the sword, by famine, and by pestilence in the place where you desire to go to dwell" (Jer. 42:22). Israel thought that Jeremiah was working on behalf of Babylon, however, and the people ignored him. The officers went to Egypt, taking Jeremiah along (Jer. 43:6). Jeremiah predicted that Babylon would overtake them in Egypt and kill them there and would capture Egypt as well (Jer. 43:10–13).

Prophecies concerning the downfall of Egypt continued to be fulfilled in the later conquering of Egypt by the Medo-Persians, the Greeks under Alexander the Great, and finally Rome. Egypt fell into decline and became a minor power in much the same way all nations who have oppressed Israel eventually decline.

Scripture predicts that Egypt will have a role in the future millennial kingdom. According to Isaiah 19:19 – 20, "In that day there will be an altar to the LORD in the midst of the land of Egypt, and a pillar to the LORD at its border . . . for they will cry to the LORD . . . and He will send them a Savior and a Mighty One, and He will deliver them."

Assyria

Assyria was the greatest empire of the Middle East in the seventh and eighth centuries B.C. Her armies captured the ten tribes of Israel in 722 B.C. and dominated the political scene for a century. By God's command, Jonah traveled to Nineveh, the capital of Assyria, with God's message of impending divine judgment. The people's repentance provided a basis for God to extend the life and power of Assyria for 150 years. But in 612 B.C. Nineveh fell and the power of Assyria came to an end. Like Egypt, some of the prophecies concerning Assyria have not yet been fulfilled, and she is assured a place in the prophetic future.

Babylon

According to the prophecies of Daniel, there would be four great world empires fulfilling what Luke 21:24 refers to as "the times of the Gentiles." The rising power of Babylon not only destroyed Assyria but conquered Jerusalem in the summer of 605 B.C. As a lad, Daniel was carried to Babylon as a captive and began his long life of public service there.

Daniel interpreted Nebuchadnezzar's dream, prophesying four great world empires, beginning with Babylon (Daniel 2). Daniel saw the same truth revealed in the figure of four beasts in the vision recorded in chapter seven.

The prophecies concerning these four empires are so detailed and accurate that liberals who want to deny the truth of prophecy must also deny that Daniel wrote the book in the sixth century B.C. They claim it was written centuries later after the prophecies had been fulfilled. This view is uniformly rejected by both Jewish and Christian orthodox expositors. Babylon was one of the greatest empires in the past and will reappear in the end time both religiously and politically.

Although Babylon as an empire ceased to exist when the Medes and Persians conquered it in 539 B.C., according to prophecy the religious aspects of the Babylonian nation as well as the city of Babylon will reappear in the end time.

Babylon's religion, thrown out by the Medes and the Persians in 539 B.C., moved first of all to Pergamum (Rev. 2:12–17) and then later to Rome where it corrupted Christianity. This religion reappears in the world religion of Revelation 17:1–6. According to Revelation 16:18–19 a great earthquake will destroy the city of Babylon, whose history continues to the present day. To some extent, the final world power, which will be a revival of the Roman Empire, embodies some of the evils of the Babylonian Empire. Revelation 17:16–17 describes the destruction of Babylon as a religious system. Many Old Testament passages predict the destruction of Babylon the city, such as Isaiah 13:19–22 and Jeremiah 50:1–51:64, which saw partial fulfillment in the actions of the Medo-Persians. Babylon's complete devastation awaits future fulfillment in connection with Christ's second coming (Rev. 18:1–24).

Medo-Persia

The great city of Babylon fell in October 539 B.C. to the armies of the Medes and the Persians (Dan. 2:39; 7:5; 8:1 – 7, 20). For the next two hundred years the Medo-Persian empire held power. Daniel 5 describes the fall of Babylon and the events leading to the rise in power of this empire. Daniel 2:39 describes the empire's rule as the upper part of the body, Daniel 7:5 identifies it as a bear with three ribs in its mouth, and Daniel 8:1 – 7 and verse 20 call it a ram with two horns.

Greece

The Medes and the Persians fell to the armies of Alexander the Great, the king of Macedonia, about 331 B.C. Daniel's prophecy of this event describes the new ruling power as the lower part of the body of the image of Daniel 2:39, a leopard with four heads and four wings (Dan. 7:6), and a goat with a single horn (Dan. 8:5–8). Daniel named Greece (the successor to Macedonia) as the third of the four empires he described (Dan. 8:21). Chapter 11, verses 1–35, gives the details of the Medo-Persian and Grecian empires in a remarkable passage describing 135 specific prophecies, all of which have now been fulfilled. Nowhere else in Scripture is so much detail compressed in so few verses providing so eloquent a testimony to the accuracy of prophetic truth.

The Roman Empire

The greatest of all the empires of the past was the Roman Empire. Daniel's prophecies do not refer to it by name, but it is clearly the empire that would follow Greece. It is the legs and feet of the image of Daniel 2:40–43, the beast with great iron teeth of Daniel 7, verses 7 and 19–26, and the last empire of the times of the Gentiles. It is by far the most significant of the empires of Bible prophecy because Christ lived under its power and died at the order of a Roman ruler. With His death the previous dispensation of the Law was replaced by the Covenant of Grace.

The Roman Empire's rule extended almost seventeen hundred years, although the first seven hundred were the most significant. It began its conquests about 250 B.C. and the final Roman ruler, who ruled in name only, died in A.D. 1453. The mighty power of Rome had more influence on culture, literature, architecture, and law than any of the preceding empires.

It came into existence more than two hundred years after Daniel died. Therefore, his prophecies are important in understanding the role the Roman empire would play in future times. He described this great power as the legs and feet of the image of Daniel 2; however, more significant prophecies are recorded in Daniel 7 and in the book of Revelation. Daniel 7:7 says, "After this I saw in the night visions, and behold, [there was] a fourth beast, dreadful and terrible, exceedingly strong. It had huge iron teeth; it was devouring, breaking in pieces, and trampling the residue with its feet. It was different from all the beasts that were before it."

Like a gigantic beast with iron teeth, at the zenith of its power the armies of Rome would smash a country, carry off the able-bodied men as slaves, and leave a detachment of soldiers to enforce the collection of taxes and Roman rules of government. At its height, this empire extended its rule over Southern Europe, Northern Africa, and Western Asia. Like the earlier empires, Rome's power ran its course and declined, and the prophecies were fulfilled.

The last phrase of Daniel 7:7, however, contains a prophecy concerning the Roman empire that has not been fulfilled: "and it had ten horns." Verse 24 explains that "the ten horns are ten kings who shall arise from this kingdom." There is no room for speculation. The ten horns clearly are rulers of ten countries. Since no such arrangement has ever existed in the history of the Roman Empire, this reemergence must take place in the future.

This prophecy, like many others in the Old Testament, skips from the first century to immediately before the end time, without mentioning the present age. The reference to ten horns indicates that the revival of the Roman Empire will occur in the end time when ten nations will be banded together. These nations will likely come from the territory occupied by the ancient Roman Empire. Though not named, presumably the liaison will include Italy, the capital country of the Roman Empire. Others, such as Spain, France, and Greece, and possibly some nations from Western Asia and Northern Africa will likely be included. This ten-nation empire will probably emerge after the rapture of the church.

In Daniel 7:8, Daniel describes the ruler of this new empire: "I was considering the horns, and there was another horn, a little one, coming up among them, before whom three of the first horns were plucked out by the roots. And there, in this horn, were eyes like the eyes of a man, and a mouth speaking pompous words." This passage is easier to understand than other prophecies because it describes a male ruler who conquers three of the ten countries and then, apparently, will gain control of the other seven, although Daniel 7 does not say so specifically. This ruler will become the strong man in the Middle East, something missing from that region for centuries. This

man is referred to by other titles elsewhere in the Old
Testament as well as in the New Testament. Daniel 7:23
indicates he will be the final world ruler and will conquer
the entire earth:

> The fourth beast shall be
> A fourth kingdom on earth,
> Which shall be different from all other kingdoms,
> And shall devour the whole earth,
> Trample it and break it in pieces.

This reference to "the whole earth" refers to the entire
globe. No where else in earlier Scripture do we find another reference of this kind, though the whole world is in
view in many later prophecies.

The little horn of Daniel 7:8 is the willful king of Daniel
11:36 who will participate in the final world war prior to
the Second Coming. Daniel 9:24–27 describes the 490
years of Israel's prophecy and predicts that this ruler will
dominate the last seven years (Dan. 7:8). The New International translation of Daniel 9:26–27 is very confusing
and contradictory, but other translations are better. The
New King James Version reads,

> And after the sixty-two weeks
> Messiah shall be cut off, but not for Himself;
> And the people of the prince who is to come
> Shall destroy the city and the sanctuary.

The "prince who is to come" is the one person who will
"confirm a covenant" (v. 27). This man should not be
confused with Jesus Christ, who is the Messiah, or "the
Anointed One" of Daniel 9:25 (NIV). The confusion arises
when the NIV refers to the ruler as the Anointed One. The
NIV's translation tends to support the amillennial view
that other translations, such as the *New King James, King
James*, and *New American Standard*, do not recognize.
This future ruler is the one who, according to Daniel 9:27,
"shall confirm a covenant with many for one week; but in
the middle of the week He shall bring an end to sacrifice
and offering."

In the New Testament this ruler is called "the man of

sin" in 2 Thessalonians 2:3, who will set himself up as God in the final Great Tribulation (v. 4). The man of sin is also linked to, although not specifically called, the Antichrist. The final world ruler is anti-Christ in the sense that he will be against Christ. He will also be the one who will try to take Christ's place as King of kings and Lord of lords.

Revelation 13 provides the most detailed account of this final ruler's reign. He will have power "against the saints and to conquer them. And he was given authority over every tribe, people, language and nation" (Rev. 13:7 NIV). Furthermore, according to Revelation 13:8, people will worship him as God.

His reign of power will begin when he conquers the ten nations. Then he will impose a seven-year covenant on Israel (Dan. 9:27). The last half of this reign will be the Great Tribulation when he serves as world ruler, claims to be God, and allies himself with Satan.

The prediction of a future world government is especially timely today when our world leaders are discussing the future of the United Nations. Some believe the UN will eventually become a world empire. That is a significant consideration because, for the first time in history, a world government is actually feasible. To succeed, such a government would require rapid transportation, instant communication, and other methods to maintain control, such as a giant computer that could control the world's economy. A world ruler would also need an instant and effective method of controlling missile warfare in order to keep the world cowed by his power. Such was not possible before the twentieth century, but recent advancements in technology make these methods possible. Transporting armaments during the Gulf War was rapid enough to prevent the Iraqis from invading other countries. As recently as World War II, such rapid movement of men and equipment was impossible. Just fifty years ago all such shipments were made by boat, a means much too slow to deter a determined military invasion of the Middle East.

The world today awaits these events, believing that

some will occur in our present generation, although the Bible does not give grounds for dating the fulfillment of prophecy. (For further discussion see chapters 10 and 11.)

The Seventh Empire

According to Daniel 7, verses 13–14 and 26–27, when the Son of Man returns to earth at the Second Coming, the final form of the Roman Empire will be destroyed. The seventh great empire is Christ's thousand-year reign over both Jews and Gentiles. These events are described in Revelation 20 (and will be discussed at length in Chapter 12).

The seventh empire will merge with the new heaven and the new earth and will remain for eternity. The Second Coming will end the times of the Gentiles (Luke 21:24), deliver Jerusalem from Gentile oppression forever, assure the restoration of the people of Israel, as well as extend blessings to the Gentiles numbered among the saved during Christ's thousand-year reign.

Some of the confusion in understanding prophecy of the millennial kingdom arises from the fact that throughout the Old Testament prophecies of the coming Messiah often seem to imply that He would come only once. In surveying the Old Testament and Gospel periods, it is clear that no one during those times understood the Messiah would come twice in two separate events. Because they thought the Messiah would appear on earth only once, the Jewish rabbis were puzzled, wondering how He could be both a suffering Savior and a glorious, reigning Lord of lords and King of kings. The first chapter of 1 Peter, verses 10 and 11, addresses the difficulty the people had in understanding the prophecies: "Concerning this salvation, the prophets, who spoke of the grace that was to come to you, searched intently and with the greatest care, trying to find out the time and circumstances to which the Spirit of Christ in them was pointing when he predicted the sufferings of Christ and the glories that would follow" (NIV).

How could "the sufferings of Christ" and "the glories that would follow" refer to the same person? Some Jewish rabbis, unable to understand, suggested there must be two Messiahs, one who would suffer and one who would reign gloriously. During His public ministry, Christ did not attempt to solve this problem, although He did describe in great detail His second coming and His triumphant judgment of a wicked world.

Matthew 24 records what Christ told His disciples of these events, but it is doubtful that they understood until after His ascension following His death and resurrection. The disciples realized then that they had seen the prophecies of His suffering fulfilled, but not the prophecies of His glorious reign. They finally understood that those would be fulfilled in the future.

Today students of the Old Testament have no difficulty detecting the difference between these two events because they realize that any passages dealing with the sufferings of Christ refer to His first coming, and passages concerning His glorious reign are related to the Second Coming.

A similar confusion exists today concerning the rapture of the Church, which Christ announced to His disciples (John 14:2–3), and His second coming. This is different, however, because many believers separate the two events. We understand the Rapture as an event when Christ will take the Church out of the world and the Second Coming as His return to earth, accompanied by the saints and angels, to take over the world, judge the wicked, and establish His millennial kingdom.

God's Purpose for the Gentiles

Throughout Gentile history we see God revealed as sovereign. He has judged each empire in His time. Their rebellion described in Psalm 2 will conclude at the second coming of Christ. In dealing with the Gentile nations, God has saved and will continue to save some individuals, giving the Gentiles a time of special blessing in the body of Christ—the Church of the present age.

5

THE FIFTH KEY

Satan and His Angels

Scripture traces the origin of evil in a world ruled by a holy and righteous God to the spiritual fall of Satan and the angels who joined him in rebellion. This occurred long before mankind was created.

Who Is Satan?

Before God began the creation of the universe and mankind, He created a host of angels. One of them was Lucifer, who was entrusted with a high place of honor in the angelic world. Lucifer was a personality of great power, but he rebelled against God. Isaiah 14:13–14 describes Lucifer's sin. Lucifer said: "I will exalt my throne above the stars of God; . . . I will ascend above the heights of the clouds, I will be like the Most High." Other angels followed Lucifer in his rebellion and God cast them out of heaven.

The Bible refers to Lucifer more than fifty times as Satan. In the New Testament, in about thirty-three instances, he is named as "the devil." He is also identified as "a serpent," and he appeared to Adam and Eve in the Garden of Eden in that form. Fourteen times the book of Revelation calls Satan "the dragon."

From the context of these references we know that Satan and his demons are responsible for evil in the world and that evil began when he tempted Adam and Eve in the Garden, luring them into sinning against God and obeying him.

The Fall of Satan

Two major passages, Isaiah 14:12 – 15 and Ezekiel
28:11 – 19, describe Satan's fall. Both passages are warn-
ings directed at earthly kings—Sennacherib, the king of
Assyria, and the king of Tyre—prophesying their descent
into hell. But from all that Scripture and history reveal,
from the early church until now, these passages appear to
have double meanings. They refer not only to the damna-
tion of two earthly kings, but to Satan's as well.

Isaiah 14:12, directed to Sennacherib as a warning, calls
Satan "Lucifer, son of the morning," saying he has "fallen
from heaven" and is "cast down to the earth" (NIV). Verse
15 is a prophecy of Satan's final judgment: "Yet you shall
be brought down to Sheol, to the lowest depths of the Pit."

Ezekiel 28 is addressed to the king of Tyre, a great ruler
who fell from his position of power because of evil. As in
Isaiah 14, this passage describes not just the power of a
human king, but also Satan's, whose evil is the real power
behind this man's throne.

You were the seal of perfection,
Full of wisdom and perfect in beauty.
You were in Eden, the garden of God;
Every precious stone was your covering:
The sardius, topaz, and diamond,
Beryl, onyx, and jasper,
Sapphire, turquoise, and emerald with gold.
The workmanship of your timbrels and pipes
Was prepared for you on the day you were created.
You were the annointed cherub who covers;
I established you;
You were on the holy mountain of God;
You walked back and forth in the midst of fiery stones.
You were perfect in your ways from the day you were
created,
Till iniquity was found in you.
By the abundance of your trading
You became filled with violence within,
And you sinned;
Therefore I cast you as a profane thing
Out of the mountain of God;

And I destroyed you, O covering cherub,
From the midst of the fiery stones.
Your heart was lifted up because of your beauty;
You corrupted your wisdom for the sake of your splendor;
I cast you to the ground,
I laid you before kings,
That they might gaze at you.
You defiled your sanctuaries
By the multitude of your iniquities,
By the iniquity of your trading;
Therefore I brought fire from your midst;
It devoured you,
And I turned you to ashes upon the earth
In the sight of all who saw you.
All who knew you among the peoples are astonished at you;
You have become a horror,
And shall be no more forever.   (28:12–19)

Clearly this passage describes more than the sin of the
king of Tyre. The king of Tyre was not in the Garden of
Eden, but Satan was (v. 13). The king of Tyre was not a
cherub nor was he on the holy mountain of God (v. 14), but
Satan was. Like the king of Tyre, Satan will ultimately
face judgment and "will be tormented day and night forever and ever" (Rev. 20:10).

The angels who followed Satan in his rebellion were
originally holy. When they chose to follow Satan and were
cast out of heaven, they became demons. The Scriptures
often refer to the demon world and their ultimate judgment. However, God did not allow all of them into the
earthly world with Satan. Some of them He confined
immediately. Second Peter 2:4 states, "For if God did not
spare the angels who sinned, but cast them down to hell
and delivered them into chains of darkness, to be reserved
for judgment," then God is righteous in judging wicked
men as well. He condemned Sodom and Gomorrah "to
destruction, making them an example to those who afterward would live ungodly" (v. 6). According to the sixth
verse of Jude, "The angels who did not keep their proper
domain, but left their own habitation, He has reserved in
everlasting chains under darkness for the judgment of the

great day."

From these references, it becomes clear that Satan was originally a holy angel who fell into sin, and he is a personality of great power whom God has allowed to continue his rebellion to the present hour. Although much of the revelation concerning Satan is now history, he will also play an important roll in the fulfillment of other prophecies, especially those leading to the Second Coming. Satan's activities reveal him as the personification of evil. Therefore, any denial of Satan's existence, his person, or his work does violence to scriptural revelation. His character and his work do much to explain the presence of evil in God's world. And the revelation of Satan and his activities found in the Old and New Testaments forms an important background to the great prophecies that relate Satan to end-time events.

Satan's Evil Work

The book of Job describes God's challenge to Satan to observe Job's piety and faithfulness, saying, "There is none like him on the earth, a blameless and upright man, one who fears God and shuns evil" (1:8). Satan asked, "Does Job fear God for nothing?" (1:9). Then Satan tried to argue that Job wasn't inherently good but only appeared to be blameless because God had protected him from temptation: "Have You not made a hedge around him, around his household, and around all that he has on every side? You have blessed the work of his hands, and his possessions have increased in the land. But now, stretch out Your hand and touch all that he has, and he will surely curse You to Your face!" (1:10–11).

Satan wanted to afflict Job seriously to prove to God that no man is blameless and upright, that no man will fear God and shun evil when he is suffering. In other words, Satan believed that when the pain is great enough all mankind will turn from God and follow him. In his providence God knew what Job would do, and He allowed Satan to test him by taking away Job's wealth and, except

for his wife, all of his family. The most significant factor
in Job's experience is that Satan could not afflict Job
without God's permission.

But Job maintained his fidelity and his faith in God, and
Satan challenged God again, proposing to bring affliction
on Job's body, saying, "Yes, all that a man has he will give
for his life. But stretch out Your hand now, and touch his
bone and his flesh, and he will surely curse You to Your
face" (2:4–5). God granted Satan permission to further
afflict Job, but He prohibited Satan from taking Job's life
(2:6).

This experience makes clear that while Satan has great
power, God limits that power. Yet, although God protects
believers from Satan's work to some extent, still sometimes they face severe trials.

The book of Job is the history of Satan's evil work
against one righteous man. The Old Testament also records Satan's attacks on others, revealing that Satan can
have an evil influence even on a child of God. First
Chronicles 21:1 records Satan working against David:
"Satan stood up against Israel, and moved David to number Israel." David allowed Satan to influence him. He
sent Joab out to take a census and "God was displeased
with this thing" (21:7). God judged David for his sin.
Zechariah 3:1–2 shows Joshua in God's presence and
Satan, the adversary, is there also. God rebukes Satan,
reminding him "Is this not a brand plucked from the fire?"
(v. 2). Even though God will allow Satan and his evil work,
God remains supreme over Satan.

Most of the biblical references to demons are in the New
Testament, but there are some in the Old Testament that
are significant. In Deuteronomy 32:17 Moses speaks of
the people making sacrifices to demons and, according to
Psalm 106:37, "They even sacrificed their sons / And their
daughters to demons." Although the Old Testament
makes few references to demons, obviously demon activity
was behind the people's worshiping idols.

Many of the New Testament references to demons are

in the Gospels where we find the record of about thirty instances of demon possession. Many of the demon possessed were brought to Christ, who cast out the evil spirits (Matt. 4:24; 8:16; 12:22). The epistles also mention demons, but not in terms of demon possession. Because no revelation of demons possessing a Christian is included, the New Testament implies that when the Spirit indwells a person, demon possession cannot occur. But the New Testament makes clear that Christians can be demon oppressed.

The work of Satan is revealed in a number of New Testament passages. In Matthew 4 the devil tempts Christ and tries to divert Him from His perfect obedience to God. In Matthew 13:39, Satan sows "tares" to compete with the "good seed" sown by Christ. In John 8, verses 48 and 52, Christ's enemies accuse Him of being demon possessed. Satan's work in keeping people from receiving the Word of God is all too plain, as revealed for example, in the fourth chapter of Mark. When people hear the word of God, "Satan comes immediately and takes away the word that was sown in their hearts" (v. 15). Judas Iscariot's betrayal of Christ is another illustration of how Satan can work in the heart of a man (John 13:2). In later passages the Bible says that Satan entered Judas (Luke 22:3; see also John 13:27).

Throughout the New Testament Satan is revealed as a deceiving angel of light (2 Cor. 11:14) and the power behind the future Antichrist (Rev. 13:2). In the future millennial kingdom, God will bind Satan and the demon world for all of the thousand years of Christ's millennial reign. At the end, before they are finally cast into the lake of fire, Satan and his evil angels will be released (Rev. 20:1 – 3, 7 – 10).

The pattern Satan follows in tempting all Christians is the same as his temptation of Christ. He uses "the cravings of sinful man, the lust of his eyes, and the boasting of what he has and does" (1 John 2:16 NIV). Christ faced "the cravings of sinful man" when Satan tempted Him to turn

stones to bread after His forty days of fasting (Matt. 4:3).
When Satan held out to Christ all the glory of the world's
kingdoms (v. 9), he was appealing to the "lust" of the eyes.
In challenging Christ to cast Himself down from the temple so people would bow to Him as God (v. 6), Satan was
appealing to human pride or boasting. Because Christ did
not have a sinful nature and because He was God, He could
not be tempted. However, in spite of God's salvation,
Christians do have sinful natures. When Satan uses his
methods against us, we can be tempted.

Satan and the Cross of Christ

Christ's death on the cross seemed to be a major victory
for Satan, because he had brought about the death of the
Son of God. However, Christ's death actually gloriously
defeated Satan because it unlocked God's grace. John
16:8 – 13 reveals how the Holy Spirit would convict mankind after Christ's return to heaven and foretells that the
Spirit of truth will come to "guide you into all truth."
According to verse 11, "The prince of this world [Satan]
now stands condemned" (NIV). The glory in the cross is that
multitudes will be saved throughout history and, ultimately, Satan himself will be judged.

The cross of Christ brings reconciliation for the hearts
of those who trust Him. At present Satan is a condemned
criminal whose execution has not taken place, but his final
judgment is sure. Meanwhile those who trust in Christ
can have victory over Satan.

Prophecy of Satan's Future

Satan will figure prominently in end-time events because he will be the power behind the future world ruler,
as well as the opposition to God that will characterize the
Great Tribulation. Revelation 12:7–9 contains the major
prophecy of Satan's role in those events: "And war broke
out in heaven: Michael and his angels fought with the
dragon; and the dragon and his angels fought, but they did
not prevail, nor was a place found for them in heaven any
longer. So the great dragon was cast out, that serpent of

old, called the Devil and Satan, who deceives the whole
world; he was cast to the earth, and his angels were cast
out with him."

The prophecy says that Satan will have great wrath:
"Woe to the inhabitants of the earth and the sea! For the
devil has come down to you, having great wrath, because
he knows that he has a short time" (v. 12). For three and
a half years (Rev. 12:6, 14; Dan. 7:25) God will allow Satan
to continue his evil work on earth, until the second coming
of Christ. But at the beginning of Christ's thousand-year
reign on earth, Satan will be bound: "Then I saw an angel
coming down from heaven, having the key to the bottomless pit and a great chain in his hand. He laid hold of the
dragon, that serpent of old, who is the Devil and Satan,
and bound him for a thousand years; and he cast him into
the bottomless pit, and shut him up, and set a seal on him,
so that he should deceive the nations no more till the
thousand years were finished. But after these things he
must be released for a little while" (Rev. 20:1–3).

For the thousand-year reign of Christ, sin will still
operate in the world because man will still have a sinful
nature. Nevertheless, there will be no satanic activity
until the thousand years end. Satan's career will close,
however, as indicated in Revelation 20:7–10, when he is
loosed from prison. He will arouse opposition to God and
his followers will surround the city of Jerusalem. Fire
from heaven will devour them and Satan himself will be
cast into the lake of fire where he will be "tormented day
and night forever and ever" (v. 10).

Understanding the biblical knowledge of Satan—his
past, present, and future—is essential to understanding
evil in the world, salvation for those who trust in Christ,
and God's ultimate victory over and judgment on every evil
thing.

6

THE SIXTH KEY

Israel

No area of eschatology has been more important in the history of the Church than prophecy about Israel. The confusion existing today over prophetic interpretation stems largely from failure to understand these predictions.

Evidence points to the conclusion that for the first two centuries the early church held the premillennial interpretation of Scripture. Believers of that time embraced the belief that Christ will return and begin a thousand-year reign on earth during which time Israel will be prominent. However, opposition to this interpretation arose during the last decade of the second century and for the first time some scholars professed a belief that denies the literal fulfillment of prophecy concerning the future of Israel. The School of Theology in Alexandria, Egypt, developed these opposing interpretations, leading to amillennialism and postmillennialism.

Because Israel is a major subject of prophecy in both the Old and New Testaments, the idea that prophecies about this nation will not be literally fulfilled was a major stumbling block to coherent prophetic interpretation. The continuing controversy underscores the fact that unless a person understands God's program for Israel, he will not understand God's distinctive program for the Church or for the world. One cannot choose to interpret some prophecies in one way (literally) and others in another (nonliterally) and hope to find the truth inherent in all prophecies. Because the Bible is God's Word and His Word is dependable, prophecy concerning Israel is a vital foundation for all other prophecy and an important facet for understanding future events. The key to Israel's future is in God's covenant with Abraham which was an important new development in the revelation of the divine prophetic program.

With this covenant, God began a special program that set Abraham and his descendants apart from the Gentile world.

The Abrahamic Covenant

The promises God made to Abraham are outlined in Genesis 12:1–3: Abraham's name would be great, God would bless him, he would father a great nation, and through him all families of the earth would be blessed. In addition, God promised He would bless those who blessed Abraham and curse those who cursed him.

Abraham, who was childless, suggested that God name Eliezer of Damascus, Abraham's favorite servant, as his son (Gen. 15:2). As Eliezer had children, Abraham would have heirs. But God rejected Abraham's suggestion, saying, "This one shall not be your heir, but one who will come from your own body shall be your heir." Then God brought Abraham outside and said, "Look now toward heaven, and count the stars if you are able to number them. . . . So shall your descendants be" (vv. 4–5).

According to Scripture, Abraham "believed in the LORD," and because Abraham believed, God "accounted it to him for righteousness" (v. 6). Abraham had no hard evidence that God's Word would be fulfilled. He had only faith on which to base his belief. Abraham is a compelling illustration of a righteous man who trusted God in all things.

Over time God assured Abraham again and again that he would have an heir, but still Abraham was childless. Abraham's wife, wanting Abraham to have children, took

matters into her own hands. She offered her maid to
Abraham to be a wife to him and give him children. And
Abraham "heeded the voice" of his wife (16:2). The maid,
Hagar, bore Abraham a son, Ishmael. But this was not
the fulfillment of God's promise, nor was Ishmael to be a
part of the covenant God had made with Abraham.

The fact that Abraham and Sarah, his wife, tried to
"help" God fulfill the promise that Abraham would have a
son is considered by some as Abraham's sin and an indication of his lack of faith. But actually it shows that this
righteous man, who would become the father of a great
nation, was a man. Much like all mankind since the
beginning of time, Abraham wanted to understand God's
promises in human terms. He considered himself and
Sarah old—she was far too old to produce a child from her
own body. We can certainly assume that in His divine
wisdom God knew what they would do and allowed it in
order to demonstrate to Abraham and Sarah, and all who
would follow, that His promises are dependable and will
be literally fulfilled, in spite of human constraints.

When Abraham was ninety-nine years of age, except for
Ishmael he was still childless. God repeated His promise:

> I am Almighty God; walk before Me and be blameless. And
> I will make My covenant between Me and you, and will
> multiply you exceedingly. . . . As for Me, behold, My
> covenant is with you, and you shall be a father of many
> nations. No longer shall your name be called Abram, but
> your name shall be Abraham; for I have made you a father
> of many nations. I will make you exceedingly fruitful; and
> I will make nations of you, and kings shall come from you.
> And I will establish My covenant between Me and you and
> your descendants after you in their generations, for an
> everlasting covenant, to be God to you and your descen-
> dants after you.   (17:1–7)

Then God added a promise concerning Sarah:

> I will bless her and also give you a son by her; then I will
> bless her, and she shall be a mother of nations; kings of
> peoples shall be from her."   (v. 16)

When Abraham expressed unbelief and begged God to

allow Ishmael to be his heir, God said, "No, Sarah your wife shall bear you a son, and you shall call his name Isaac; I will establish My covenant with him for an everlasting covenant, and with his descendants after him" (v. 19). But Sarah was also human and wanted to understand God's promise within what she perceived to be her human capabilities. She was ninety years old. The idea that she could conceive and bear a child made her laugh. Knowing what was in her heart, God asked Abraham, "Is anything too hard for the LORD?" (18:14).

This most wonderful promise of all—that nothing is too hard for the Lord God Almighty—is the foundation of all our faith and the true basis on which all prophecy rests. From it we know that all God's promises will be fulfilled completely.

At the "appointed time" and "according to the time of life" (v. 14), God returned to Abraham and Sarah and the prophecy concerning Isaac's birth was meticulously and literally fulfilled. Ishmael would not inherit the covenant God made with Abraham, but God promised to bless him and "make him fruitful" and "multiply him exceedingly." Ishmael would "beget twelve princes" and God would "make him a great nation" (17:20). God also reinforced the promise He had made to Abraham earlier that Israel would possess the land to which Abraham had come (see 12:7; 13:14–17; 15:18–21; and 17:8).

The promise of Genesis 12:3 includes details of Abraham's future blessing and God's promise to bless those who would bless Abraham's posterity and curse those who would not. This promise has been graphically fulfilled in history. Every nation that has persecuted Israel has paid a price, beginning with Egypt, then Assyria, Babylon, Medo-Persia, and Greece, and finally, Rome. In more recent times Russia, Germany, Spain, and other countries have persecuted the nation of Israel and have suffered diminished power and world prestige. In contrast, America and the countries that have been relatively kind to Israel have enjoyed continued power and prosperity.

The promise that a great nation would come from Abraham is important in the revelation of God's plan for Israel. The promise involved numerous details that are unfolded and subsequently confirmed in Scripture (Gen. 13:14–17; 15:1–7, 18–21; 17:1–8). These passages foretold that Israel would become a great nation (12:2), and the promise of a great nation belonged to a particular line of Abraham's descendants, specifically through Isaac and Jacob; to these descendants of Abraham belonged the everlasting possession of the promised land (17:8); the nation would continue forever and the covenant was everlasting and irrevocable (17:7); and God would be their God (17:8).

Throughout time Abraham has been a great name in both Christianity and Judaism, and Muslims regard him as a prophet as well. His example as a man of faith has been a great blessing to mankind. Miraculously Sarah gave birth to Isaac; then Jacob, Isaac's son, fathered twelve sons who established and led the twelve tribes of Israel. In addition, through Ishmael and the children Abraham had with Keturah and through Esau, Jacob's twin brother, Abraham had many descendants. Just as the prophecies promised, a great posterity descended from Abraham, but the covenant promise was completely fulfilled only through Jacob.

In the centuries since Abraham, Isaac, and Jacob, the preservation of the nation Israel has been a miracle. She has retained her identity for almost four thousand years in spite of centuries of living among the nations of the world. By looking back through history we can identify the complete and literal fulfillment of these prophecies and know with certainty that those remaining unfulfilled will come to pass in the same way completely and literally.

The Promise of the Land

Two major areas of promise to Israel relate to the Promised Land and the restoration of Israel in the period after Christ's second coming. Both of these prophecies are at the heart of the question of whether the premillennial interpretation is correct and there will be a thousand-year kingdom after the Second Coming, or the amillennial and postmillennial views are correct and there will be no millennium after the Second Coming. If there is no millennium, obviously the promise about the Land will not be fulfilled, although the spiritual restoration of Israel might be possible. Because of the importance of these items, we will consider them in detail.

God said to Abraham, "To your descendants I will give this land" (Gen. 12:7). Regardless of how obscure and symbolic some people declare prophecy to be, this statement is quite clear. There is nothing obscure or symbolic in it. In fact, it plainly states God's intention to give the Promised Land to Abraham. Previously, God had told Abraham to leave his homeland and Ur of the Chaldees and go to a land that God would show him. Once Abraham arrived there, God reaffirmed His promise that the Land would belong to Abraham's descendants.

The most common interpretation of this passage by amillenarians and postmillenarians is that "the Land" refers to heaven or another place that is not on earth. But in any case, they say it does not refer literally to the land where Abraham was living at the time. A thorough study of the Old Testament, however, does not reveal even one instance where "the Land" refers to heaven, even though the idea has been perpetuated by many of our hymns that refer to Canaan as heaven. There is simply no scriptural support for the claim that in Old Testament prophecy Canaan means heaven. A detailed survey of the Old Testament reveals that "the Land" always refers literally to land as it does in Genesis 13:14–15: "And the LORD said to Abram, after Lot had separated from him: 'Lift your eyes now and look from the place where you are—northward, southward, eastward, and westward; for all the land which you see I give to you and your descendants forever.'" Obviously what Abraham saw was real estate, and he understood that was what God was going to give him.

Later, when Abraham once again needed reassurance that God would give him a son, Scripture records that God performed a sacred rite—a ceremony which included the shedding of blood—and then defined the land He was talking about: "On the same day the LORD made a covenant with Abram, saying: 'To your descendants I have given this land, from the river of Egypt to the great river, the River Euphrates—the Kenites, the Kenezzites, the Kadmonites, the Hittites, the Perizzites, the Rephaim, the Amorites, the Canaanites, the Girgashites, and the Jebusites'" (15:18–21). It is clear that the land God described was real, that Abraham could see it, and that it was physically inhabited at that time by heathen tribes God would drive out. It should also be clear that Abraham understood God was not talking about heaven, but the Promised Land to which Abraham had already literally come, and that he could see.

Genesis 17:8 further confirms that "the land" is not a symbolic reference: "Also I give to you and your descendants after you the land in which you are a stranger, all the land of Canaan, as an everlasting possession; and I will be their God."

Another confirmation that the land of God's promise was earthly land occurred when Isaac was about to flee to Egypt. God said, "Do not go down to Egypt; dwell in the land of which I shall tell you. Sojourn in this land, and I will be with you and bless you; for to you and your descendants I give all these lands, and I will perform the oath which I swore to Abraham your father" (26:2–3). At that time God revealed to Isaac that the offspring of Abraham, to whom the Land was promised, would descend from him, Abraham's son (26:4–5).

Much later, after Jacob stole Esau's birthright and was fleeing to avoid Esau's anger, God appeared to Jacob. Scripture records that God gave him a dream: "And behold, a ladder was set up on the earth, and its top reached to heaven; and there the angels of God were ascending and descending on it. And behold, the LORD stood above it and said: 'I am the LORD God of Abraham your father and the God of Isaac; the land on which you lie I will give to you and your descendants'" (28:12–13). God further promised that Jacob's posterity would inherit the Land and that he would inherit the other promises God had given Abraham. It is clear that God was reaffirming His promise to give actual land on earth to Jacob and his posterity.

Obviously the promise was not immediately fulfilled. The nation of Israel lived in Egypt for several hundred years. God warned of this when He said they would reside for a time in a land where they would be enslaved (15:13 – 14). He also said they would eventually be freed. Under Moses and Joshua, the children of Israel left Egypt to go to the Promised Land, as recorded in the book of Exodus. In spite of the unbelief that caused them to wander for forty years in the wilderness, eventually under Joshua they crossed the Jordan River and took possession of much of the Promised Land.

Before his death Moses solemnly warned Israel that if they obeyed the Law God had given them in the wilderness, He would bless them in the Land; but if they didn't, God would drive them out:

> And it shall be, that just as the LORD rejoiced over you to do you good and multiply you, so the LORD will rejoice over you to destroy you and bring you to nothing; and you shall be plucked from off the land which you go to possess. Then the LORD will scatter you among all peoples, from one end of the earth to the other, and there you shall serve other gods, which neither you nor your fathers have known— wood and stone. And among those nations you shall find no rest, nor shall the sole of your foot have a resting place; but there the LORD will give you a trembling heart, failing eyes, and anguish of soul. Your life shall hang in doubt before you; you shall fear day and night, and have no assurance of life.   (Deut. 28:63–66)

The Assyrian and Babylonian captivities (722 and 605-586 B.C.) partially fulfilled these prophecies. Ultimately, following the destruction of Jerusalem in A.D. 70, the people of Israel would scatter all over the world.

Joshua reemphasized this prophecy when he told the people what God had revealed to him: "Every place that the sole of your foot will tread upon I have given you, as I said to Moses" (Joshua 1:3). Although Israel did not possess all the land at that time, they possessed a substantial part, and for the next seven hundred years the nation enjoyed the Land. However, just as Moses had warned, when once again they departed from God, they found themselves in Assyrian and later Babylonian captivity.

Jeremiah ministered to Israel in the midst of their apostasy and reassured them that after seventy years they would be released. Again, the people anticipated the literal fulfillment of prophecy. Jeremiah 29:10 reveals God's words: "After seventy years are completed at Babylon, I will visit you and perform My good word toward you, and cause you to return to this place."

Sixty-seven years later, the captive Daniel somehow secured the manuscript of Jeremiah's prophecy and turned to prayer and confession, claiming God's fulfillment of the promise. Daniel believed the prophecy about the Land would be fulfilled literally.

The actual return is recorded in the book of Ezra. Fifty thousand Israelites went back to begin to reinhabit the Land. Their return resulted in the literal fulfillment of another prophecy: Christ was born in Bethlehem, a suburb of Jerusalem, and not in Babylon, in fulfillment of the prophecy concerning the birth place of the Messiah found in Micah 5:2.

The scattering of Israel all over the world after A.D. 70 caused many biblical scholars to decide the nation would never be reassembled in the Promised Land. They made these predictions in spite of the very clear and specific promises that Israel will return (Jer. 23:5–8; Amos 9:11–15; Ezek. 39:25–29). Scripture declares Christ will return and occupy the throne of David (Ps. 89:3–4, 19–37), and that when He does, Israel will be regathered to her Land. Accordingly, God revealed to Jeremiah, "'Therefore, behold, the days are coming,' says the LORD, 'that they shall no longer say, "As the LORD lives who brought up the children of Israel from the land of Egypt," but, "As the LORD lives who brought up and led the descendants of the house of Israel from the north country and from all the countries where I had driven them." And they shall dwell in their own land'" (Jer. 23:7–8). This promise is specific. At the second coming of Christ, when He comes to reign over Israel, He will regather the people of Israel. These promises are augmented by many other promises.

Ezekiel 39:25–29, records again the promise that God will bring the Israelites out of the nations (v. 27) and they will inhabit the Land. "Then they shall know that I am the LORD their God, who sent them into captivity among the nations, but also brought them back to their land, and left none of them captive any longer" (v. 28). Other Scripture, such as Ezekiel 20:33–38, indicates God will purge the rebels who are unbelievers and will reunite the godly remnant of Israel. Further, Ezekiel records in chapters 47 and 48 how the Lord will apportion the land to the twelve tribes (47:13–48:7).

Obviously, the promise has not been completely fulfilled and is subject to literal fulfillment in the future. As such, it is powerful proof that Israel will play a vital role in the Second Coming and the millennial kingdom.

The Restoration of the Nation

Inherent in all the prophecies concerning possessing the Land is the promise that Israel will be restored as a nation—spiritually, politically, and territorially. Just as the nation of Israel will possess the Land forever, so they will constitute a nation forever, and Christ will reign over them. Many passages in the Old Testament confirm this. Isaiah 2:1–5 describes Jerusalem as the center of the divine government with Christ ruling the world from the throne of David. Isaiah 11 speaks of the righteousness of this kingdom; verses 1–16 picture God's righteous judgment as well as the peace and tranquility which will characterize the kingdom. Psalm 72 describes the universality of His rule, and other Old Testament passages confirm these prophecies.

Although whether a particular generation would inhabit the Land depended on their obedience, God's ultimate plan to restore Israel is clear. The fulfillment of this promise is just as sure as those describing Christ's Second Coming.

Although amillenarians and others, who question the literal fulfillment of these promises, believe Israel will never again possess the Land, the facts of history do not support their nonliteral interpretation. Just as the Israelites actually went to Egypt and returned, were carried off into the captivities and returned, and scattered all over the world, so they will come back to the Land and actually inhabit it.

The Mosaic Covenant

Much of the confusion in interpreting prophecy is due to failing to distinguish between Israel and the Church. Attempts to apply the laws of the Mosaic Covenant to the Church have caused misunderstanding of God's intent in the present age of grace.

Mosaic Law provided rules for living that were in effect from the time God gave the laws to Moses until Christ's death and resurrection abolished the covenant. The new Covenant of Grace also contains rules for living, some of them going beyond the moral principles of the Mosaic Covenant, and it incorporates some principles that are a part of every dispensation.

A significant difference between the Mosaic Covenant and the new Covenant of Grace is that the Mosaic Covenant was only for Israel. Its rules and regulations for daily life applied to this life only. It did not provide a way of salvation, for eternal life in heaven was not one of its promises, neither was hell among its curses. These rules were the basis for God's dealings with Israel until the advent of the Messiah. Therefore, observing the laws was an indication of faith in the covenant God had made with the nation of Israel, not a way of salvation, and Gentiles were not a part of it.

The new Covenant of Grace is for the church established by the birth, death, and resurrection of Jesus Christ, and its promises extend to all people, Israelites and Gentiles alike. The new covenant is fully revealed in the New Testament and those morals and judgments of the Mosaic Covenant that are in the new covenant are specifically restated in the New Testament. The rules and regulations of the Mosaic Covenant that are not restated in the Covenant of Grace as revealed in the New Testament simply are not a part of the new covenant.

For example, the Ten Commandments given to Moses are all restated in the New Testament, except for the law of the Sabbath. Therefore, God does not judge the church for worshiping on the first day of the week instead of the seventh. In the same manner, He does not judge believers in the present age for failing to keep other rules for daily living that applied only to Israel before the birth of Christ.

The most significant aspect of the new Covenant of Grace is that it reveals the way of salvation, and it makes clear there is only one way. The new covenant also makes clear that it does not change the way of salvation. That has been the same from the dawn of creation and will remain the same forever. Throughout God's Word, from Genesis to the last page of Revelation, the Bible teaches only one way of salvation—through Jesus Christ. Most importantly, the new covenant makes clear that salvation is by grace, not works.

The saints in Old Testament times received salvation on credit, so to speak, as indicated in the third chapter of Romans. Paul said, "We know that whatever the law says, it says to those who are under the law, that every mouth may be stopped, and all the world may become guilty before God" (v. 19). But the righteousness of God "apart from the law is revealed . . . through faith in Jesus Christ" (vv. 21–22). Through Christ's sacrifice and death on the

cross "in His forbearance God had passed over the sins that
were previously committed, to demonstrate at the present
time His righteousness, that He might be just and the
justifier of the one who has faith in Jesus" (vv. 25–26).
Accordingly, salvation in the Old Testament is based on
the death of Christ just as it is in the New.

The letter to the Galatians settles the confusion of what
applies to Israel and what to the church. It points out that
salvation is by grace alone, not by law, and that the moral
regulations of the Old Testament cannot coexist with the
regulations in the New, except as the laws are repeated.
Paul demonstrates the incompatibility of the two systems
using the two wives of Abraham to illustrate. The slave
woman from Egypt, Hagar, and Sarah, the free woman,
could not coexist, and the slave woman's son was driven
out. "These things may be taken figuratively," Paul said,
"for the women represent two covenants. One covenant is
from Mount Sinai and bears children who are to be slaves:
This is Hagar. Now Hagar stands for Mount Sinai in
Arabia and corresponds to the present city of Jerusalem,
because she is in slavery with her children. But the
Jerusalem that is above is free, and she is our mother"
(4:24–26 NIV). Paul also states that in the present age
those who are members of the church, the body of Christ,
are "children of promise," just as Isaac was a child of
promise (v. 28). When God instructed Abraham to "Cast
out the bondwoman and her son, for the son of the bondwoman shall not be heir with the son of the freewoman"
(4:30; see also Gen. 21:10), He was also establishing a
foundation for the Covenant of Grace in effect during this
present age. Under the new covenant believers are born
of the Spirit and, therefore, are freed from the Law.

Second Corinthians 3:6–18 makes a similar contrast
between law and grace. This passage declares the Law is
"passing away" (v. 11). Unlike the limited revelation of
the Old Testament, the Christian comes into the fuller
revelation of the New Testament (vv. 15–18). Christ
stated this simply, saying, "For the law was given through

Moses, but grace and truth came through Jesus Christ"
(John 1:17). We should observe the similarity of the morality of Mosaic Law to the morality of the new covenant.
At the same time, however, we must recognize the absolute differences in the two rules of life.

The Davidic Covenant

<u>The Promise of a King</u>

God also made a covenant with David that included a
prophecy for the nation of Israel as well as for David's
throne. Concerning "My people Israel," God said, "I will
appoint a place . . . and will plant them, that they may
dwell in a place of their own and move no more; nor shall
the sons of wickedness oppress them anymore" (2 Sam.
7:10). Then God promised David that his throne would
endure forever (vv. 12–16). This promise is twofold. The
first part (vv.12–15) concerns an earthly throne, the sym-
bol of an earthly rule over the people of Israel. The
fulfillment would occur through time as David's descendants assumed the throne and ruled the people.

God revealed an important part of the fulfillment of this
promise to the prophet Hosea who made clear that David's
throne could be unoccupied for a time: "For the children of
Israel shall abide many days without king or prince,
without sacrifice or sacred pillar, without ephod or tera-
phim" (Hosea 3:4).

Discussions of scriptural doctrine sometimes confuse
the earthly throne of David with the kingdom of God, but
the two kingdoms are entirely different. The theocratic
kingdom, which began with David ruling over Israel, was
a throne on earth that David and his descendants occupied. It was a political rule over the children of Israel,
some of whom were saved and some of whom were not.
Central to the kingdom of God is the throne in heaven on
which Christ is now seated. The idea that this heavenly
throne is the Davidic throne is a confusion of the spiritual
kingdom of God and the theocratic kingdom of David.

In part the confusion comes from the second part of the

covenant with David, promising, "Your house and your kingdom shall be established forever before you. Your throne shall be established forever" (2 Sam. 7:16). The cornerstone of the amillennial view is that the heavenly throne from which Christ now rules in this present age is David's throne. Of course, amillenarians do not regard fulfillment of the Davidic Covenant as an essential factor in the Second Coming. Their interpretations do not allow for a premillennial kingdom and, therefore, they try to impose the spiritual kingdom of God on prophecies concerning the theocratic kingdom of David.

Premillenarians point to the consistent testimony throughout the Old Testament that the Davidic throne will be brought back, the nation of Israel will be regathered on the Land, and Christ will assume this earthly throne following the Second Coming. Jeremiah 23 and Psalm 89 quite forcefully state this. Therefore, the fulfillment of the Davidic Covenant will not establish God's new spiritual kingdom, but will continue David's earthly kingdom.

Sometimes the confusion in interpreting the prophecy of David's throne enduring forever comes from the fact that Christ is the appointed son of David who will rule on the throne. The confusion is compounded by the idea that Jesus is ruling from David's throne now from heaven. What should be more clear, however, is that Christ is not ruling theocratically over Israel today, just as His reign over the church is not theocratic, but spiritual.

Like David who was anointed king over Israel many years before he actually began his reign, so Christ is the anointed Son of David now. The prophecy of His actual reign will not be fulfilled until His second coming.

The fact that Christ rules *spiritually* over the hearts of men and will bring spiritual renewal to Israel is not sufficient fulfillment of the prophecy concerning David's throne. Through Jeremiah, God promised the day will come when Israel will be regathered and their king, a descendant of David, will reign over them. His name will be called *the Lord our Righteousness* (Jer. 23:5–6). Christ himself will fulfill this promise.

Many important Scripture passages confirm the promise of an earthly government and are clear that this is the throne of David, not the throne of God in heaven, and that this future kingdom must be related to the return of Israel to the land when Christ will reign over them (Ps. 89:36–37; Isa. 9:6–7; Jer. 23:1–8; Luke 1:31–32).

The fact that Christ will continue to be the King of Israel throughout eternity fulfills the unending character of the millennial kingdom prophesied in Daniel 7:14:

> His dominion is an everlasting dominion,
> Which shall not pass away,
> And His kingdom the one
> Which shall not be destroyed.

The kingdom promises given David mesh with the promise to Abraham that the nation Israel will continue forever and have everlasting possession of the Land. As other Scripture bears out, the present earth will be destroyed and followed by the creation of the new heaven and the new earth. Actually, the Holy Land will not be continued in the new earth. Because Scripture indicates the earth itself has a limited duration, the promises of possession of the Land are limited. Christ's rule over Israel and over heaven, however, will continue forever. The fulfillment of these promises is in keeping with the literal character of other prophetic promises given to Israel and David.

A New Covenant for Israel

God revealed to Jeremiah that He would make a new covenant with Israel, which would supersede and replace the Mosaic Covenant (Jer. 31:31–34), and it would be specifically with Israel and Judah, not with the world as a whole. According to Jeremiah, the new covenant will be fulfilled after Israel's tribulation (30:5–7; 31:1–7, 11–14), when the people have been returned to the Land (30:1–4; 31:8–10).

In contrast to the covenant that God "made with their

fathers in the day that I took them by the hand to bring
them out of the land of Egypt" (31:32), which was written
on the tables of stone and brought condemnation to the
people of Israel, God will put the new covenant "in their
minds, and write it on their hearts" (v. 33). It will bring
them spiritual blessing for "I will be their God, and they
shall be My people" (v. 33).

An unusual characteristic of the new covenant is that it
will be fulfilled in a period of universal knowledge of God.
"No more shall every man teach his neighbor, and every
man his brother, saying, 'Know the LORD,' for they all shall
know Me" (31:34). Everyone, from the least to the greatest, will have knowledge of God (Isa. 11:9).

This provision is important for understanding prophecy
as it relates to the present world situation. We should be
clear that the new covenant with Israel is not being fulfilled now and that it involves forgiveness of sins. It is a
covenant of grace.

When we consider all the provisions of the new covenant
with Israel, we can easily understand that it cannot be
fulfilled until Christ comes again and establishes His
millennial kingdom. Other passages, such as Isaiah 61:8 –
9 and Ezekiel 37:21 – 28, confirm various details of this new
covenant and point to fulfillment in the earthly millennial
kingdom.

The New Testament reveals that the Church shares in
a new covenant stemming from the death of Christ, and
mentions it frequently in passages such as Luke 22:20; 1
Corinthians 11:25; 2 Corinthians 3:6; and Hebrews 8:8 and
9:15. Still there is some confusion. Consequently some
interpreters have taken the position that there is one new
covenant with two applications, one to Israel and one to
the Church. Others have decided there are two separate
new covenants, one for Israel and one for the Church. Still
others believe there is only one covenant and it is with
Israel. This third point of view indicates the Church will
derive its blessing only from the sacrifice of Christ. A
fourth interpretation identifies Israel as the Church of the

end time. However, that point of view requires spiritual-
ization that is not supported by the text of the covenant.

Finding the truth is quite simple. Christ's death provided a gracious promise of salvation, forgiveness, and
blessing to all who are properly related to Him. The
Church finds this fulfillment in the present age. Israel
will find it in the millennial kingdom. The important
distinction is that the present fulfillment for the Church
is not sufficient to fulfill what is prophesied for Israel in
the millennial kingdom.

The Consummation of Israel's Program

The ultimate fulfillment of the divine purpose for Israel,
according to Scripture, will be in their regathering to the
Land, their possessing it, their enjoyment of the kingdom
reign of Christ, and their new covenant. All of this is
integral to all the great prophecies to be fulfilled in the
consummation of the age. If we interpret prophecy literally, the restoration of Israel can be seen to be fulfilled at
the time of Christ's second coming (for details, see chapter
11).

---- 7 ----

THE SEVENTH KEY

The Church

Prophecy concerning the Church relates to two separate and distinct entities—Christendom, or the organized church, and the spiritual entity we call "the body of Christ." Therefore, we need to understand these prophecies as they apply to the Church in these two distinct ways.

Christendom is the visible body of professing Christians that is the organized church, whether Roman Catholic, Greek Orthodox, or Protestant. It includes those who are true believers in Christ, as well as those who outwardly profess to follow Him, but have not actually received salvation.

The Church as a spiritual entity is the body of Christ. It is composed only of true believers, those who are united by eternal life and have been baptized together by the Spirit into a living organism. The body of Christ is all Christians who are actually saved, those true followers of the Lord Jesus Christ who are knit together by the baptism and regeneration of the Spirit and are related to Christ as a living body is related to its head.

The prophetic program for these two aspects of the Church, while parallel in the present age, have different consummations. Understanding the differences is vital to interpreting prophecy correctly as relating to the Church now as well as in future events.

The Course of Christendom

<u>Its Character</u>

Christ revealed the character of Christendom with seven parables that are recorded in Matthew 13. These illustrations describe the three elements that always have been and always will be integral parts of the organized church: the presence of good, the presence of evil, and the presence of Israel.

Because the organized church is composed primarily of true believers, the presence of good is a significant foundation on which it was built and thrives. In the seven parables in Matthew the element of good is represented by the grain that "fell on good ground and yielded a crop" (v. 8); the "good seed" which yielded wheat (v. 24); the "one pearl of great price" (v. 46); and the good fish gathered into vessels after the bad were separated and thrown away (vv. 47–48).

The organized church is made up of human beings, and because mankind has a sinful nature, the presence of evil is always one of the elements of Christendom. In the parables of Matthew 13, the presence of evil is represented by the seed that "fell by the wayside" (v. 4), "fell on stony places" (v. 5), and "fell among thorns" (v. 7); the tares the enemy sowed among the wheat (vv. 25–26); the leaven hidden in "three measures of meal till it was all leavened" (v. 33); and the bad fish separated and thrown away before the good were gathered into vessels (vv. 47–48).

The third element, the presence of Israel in Christendom, appears to be represented in these illustrations by the treasure "hidden in a field, which a man found and hid; and for joy over it he goes and sells all that he has and buys that field" (v. 44).

The illustration of the mustard seed (vv. 31–32) foretells how Christendom would grow from a small to a great entity and would be known and recognized throughout the world. Some interpret the parable of the pearl (vv. 45–46) as a reference to the Church of the present age, which will be consummated at the Rapture. Others will become true

believers during the period between the Rapture and the
Second Coming.

While interpretations of these parables vary, Scripture
clearly sets forth the main elements comprising the character of Christendom and indicates the organized church
as an entity will remain on the earth until the end time,
even when the body of Christ is removed at the Rapture.
Ultimately the millennial kingdom and thousand-year
reign of Christ will replace the organized church.

Trend Toward Apostasy

Scripture clearly teaches the course of the organized
church will be toward apostasy rather than the postmillennialist view which holds that the church will grow
progressively better in the present age until by the end
time all are saved. Paul was especially emphatic about the
trend toward apostasy in his first letter to Timothy. He
said, "Now the Spirit expressly says that in latter times
some will depart from the faith, giving heed to deceiving
spirits and doctrines of demons" (1 Tim. 4:1). He said
these apostates would speak with "lies in hypocrisy, having their own conscience seared with a hot iron, forbidding
to marry, and commanding to abstain from foods which
God created to be received with thanksgiving by those who
believe and know the truth" (vv. 2–3). In his second letter
to Timothy, Paul spoke again of the trend toward apostasy,
saying, "The time will come when they will not endure
sound doctrine, but according to their own desires, because
they have itching ears, they will heap up for themselves
teachers; and they will turn their ears away from the
truth, and be turned aside to fables" (2 Tim. 4:3–4).

Peter had also received revelation about the trend toward apostasy. He predicted that a characteristic would
be to deny the efficacy of Christ's death: "But there were
also false prophets among the people, just as there will be
false teachers among you. They will secretly introduce
destructive heresies, even denying the sovereign Lord who
bought them—bringing swift destruction on themselves"
(2 Peter 2:1 NIV).

Most of Peter's second epistle deals with apostasy, and predicts there will be those who scoff about Christ's second coming. He said, "Scoffers will come in the last days, walking according to their own lusts, and saying, 'Where is the promise of His coming? For since the fathers fell asleep, all things continue as they were from the beginning of creation'" (2 Peter 3:3–4). As verses five and following indicate, the scoffers' unbelief will be deliberate and will ignore the supernatural character of God's activity in history.

Theological apostasy leads to moral apostasy. This is revealed by the failures of the seven churches described in the second and third chapters of Revelation. The worship of the world ruler in Revelation 13:8, the apostate church of Revelation 17:1–18, and the description of the doom and deceptions of false teachers described in 2 Peter 2:1–22 also indicate the risks of theological apostasy. Peter makes clear that apostasy is a departure from the revelation of the person of Christ, His work on the cross, His second coming, and the moral standards linked to worship and service of God.

Many believe the evil principles of bad doctrine and immorality will penetrate Christendom in the same way leaven, or yeast, works in dough to puff it up and give it the appearance of greater substance than it really has. The parable found in Matthew 13:33 suggests the "leaven" of evil will corrupt the Church by introducing unbelief (22:23–29), worldliness (22:16–21; Mark 3:6; 1 Cor. 5:6–8; 1 John 2:15–17), and empty formality in place of reality (Matt. 23:14–28).

Absolute apostasy, or total departure from the faith, is held in check in the present age by the true Church, the body of Christ, and the restraining power of the Holy Spirit. However, even the true Church can be corrupted to a degree by these doctrinal and moral problems. At the Rapture, much of what restrains evil now will be removed and apostasy will take its final form.

The World Church

According to Revelation 17, apostasy in the organized

church will take the form of a corrupt world church in the period after the true Church has been raptured. Pictured as a harlot astride a scarlet-colored beast to be identified as the political power of the time (Rev. 13:1), the world church will be universally wicked and blasphemous and will persecute all true believers in Christ (17:1): "I saw the woman, drunk with the blood of the saints and with the blood of the martyrs of Jesus" (v. 6). The figure of the woman reveals the church's spiritual adultery with the world (vv. 4–5) and represents the final chapter of the evil religion of Babylon. This evil religion will have worldwide power and will gather all the evils that characterized Babylon in the ancient world as it penetrates the church (vv. 1, 15).

As political power grows, the world church will be destroyed according to God's purpose (vv. 16–17), probably when the predicted world government begins, and will be replaced by the final form of world religion.

World Religion, the Final Form

The final form of world religion will be based on the worship of the world ruler and Satan, who will dominate the scene in the Great Tribulation (Rev. 13:8). This world ruler will fulfill the prophecy of a man who will be Satan's substitute for Jesus Christ. Many believe this man's religious character is described in Daniel 11:36–38, which declares he will take to himself the qualities of God and deny all other deities. Paul describes this ruler as "the man of sin," "the son of perdition," "the lawless one" (2 Thess. 2:1–12). Some passages may identify him as the Antichrist (1 John 2:18, 22; 2 John 1:7).

The present movement toward a world church and the advance of atheism may be the beginning of the dual form of apostate religion predicted for the end time. That religion will first take the form of the world church and then climax in the worship of a man who is Satan's substitute for Jesus Christ. At His second coming, Jesus Christ will judge religion in all its forms. The head of the world government who claims to be God is the final form of apostate religion. He and the false prophet who assists him (Rev. 13:11–18) will be cast into the lake of fire (19:20).

The True Church, the Body of Christ

A common point of view regards the Church as universal, including all believers of every age, beginning with the saints of old and extending to those living on earth at the time of the Rapture. However, the word used in the Bible that we translate as *church* is *ekklesia* and it means the professed believers in Christ of the present age. The meaning comes from the fact that in New Testament times *ekklesia* meant "an assembly." This body of believers is distinctly different from the body of all believers of every age and does not include the saints of Old Testament time, the nation Israel, or the saints who will be on earth after the Church is raptured.

Its Announcement

As recorded in Matthew 16:18, Christ declared to Peter, "I will build My church." This statement indicates the Church would be a work of Christ Himself. The word *will* means it would be a work that would take place in the future. *Build* suggests that adding individuals to the Body of Christ would require considerable time. And *My* reveals the Church would belong to Christ, because He purchased it with His blood (Acts 20:28; Eph. 5:25). *Ekklesia* indicates the Church is comprised of true believers, both Jew and Gentile, that form a new spiritual body.

Its Formation

In contrast to Israel, a nation descended from Jacob, the creation of the Church did not depend upon a physical lineage. It is a spiritual entity with characteristics peculiar to this present age only. Although Christ announced to Peter He would build the Church, it did not become a reality until the day of Pentecost with the advent and baptism of the Spirit (Acts 1:5, 8).

At least four facts support this concept:

1.   The Church is directly related to Christ's death and

is based on his finished work on the cross (Acts
20:28; Rom. 3:24–26; Col. 1:14).

2. The Church is directly related to Christ's resurrec-
    tion and receives its new life from Him (Rom. 4:25;
    Col. 3:1–3).

3. The Church is directly related to Christ's ascension
    to heaven where He is the head of the Church,
    "which is His body," as well as a new creation (2 Cor.
    5:17; Eph. 1:19–23; Heb. 7:25; 1 John 2:1).

4. The Church is regenerated, baptized, indwelt, and
    sealed by the Spirit and, therefore, could not be
    brought into existence until the advent of the Holy
    Spirit (John 1:13; Acts 1:5; 11:16; 1 Cor. 6:19–20;
    12:13; Eph. 4:30).

Its Uniqueness

God's purpose for the Church is distinct from His divine
purpose for Israel. To the Israelites alone belong the
promises pertaining to the physical seed of Abraham,
certain covenants, and Israel's prophetic program, which
includes God's dealings with the nation immediately before and after Christ's second coming. While both Israel
and the Church share the same Savior, salvation, and
promises of God's grace, in Israel God preeminently manifested His righteousness and His faithfulness. The
Church in time and eternity is the manifestation of His
grace (Eph. 2:7).

Christ's Relationship with His Church

The New Testament describes Christ's relationship
with His church and the true believers' relationship with
Him in seven distinct ways. Each role, while seemingly
different from the others, incorporates salvation and eternal life for believers. In addition, a careful study of
Christ's description of these roles provides significant
insight into the future of the Church.

Christ is the true shepherd.
The tenth chapter of John's gospel records Jesus' words

comparing His relationship to the true Church with the relationship of a shepherd to his sheep. Jesus said, "He who enters by the door is the shepherd of the sheep. To him the doorkeeper opens, and the sheep hear his voice; and he calls his own sheep by name and leads them out" (vv. 2–3). This intimate relationship is one of personal knowledge. The shepherd knows each sheep and is willing to give his life to protect each one. The sheep trust the shepherd and, knowing his voice, follow him when he calls them.

This description of the Church reveals there would be those who pretend to be shepherds, but run away when faced with difficulties: "But he who is a hireling and not the shepherd, one who does not own the sheep, sees the wolf coming and leaves the sheep and flees; and the wolf catches the sheep and scatters them. The hireling flees because he is a hireling and does not care about the sheep" (vv. 12–13).

The promises of this passage make clear that:

- Christ's love and care for the Church will be constant and all encompassing (vv. 3, 4, 11, 27, 29–30).
- Others will try to destroy the Church (vv. 1, 5, 7, 10, 12–13, 26).
- The true Church will be composed of all who believe, whether Jew or Gentile (v. 16).
- Christ will intercede at the throne of God for the Church (vv. 15, 17–18, 25, 29).
- Christ will satisfy all the needs of the Church with guidance, protection, and spiritual food (vv. 4, 10, 14–15, 27).
- All who believe in Christ and follow His voice will have eternal life (vv. 9–10, 28–29).
- There is only one way of salvation (vv. 1, 7, 10 – 11, 29–30).

Christ is the vine.

Jesus revealed His desire for a daily relationship with the Church in the passage recorded in John 15:1–17. He spoke of communion and fruitfulness that would result only if the Church as a whole and the believers who

comprise it remain constantly connected to Him in the way
a vine's branches are attached to and sustained by the
vine.

The vine is the source of life for its branches. When the
branches are damaged or cut off, they wither and die. The
gardener prunes the whole plant, removing those
branches that do not bear fruit and cutting back those that
do, to allow the plant to produce new growth and, consequently, more fruit.

Christ exhorts believers to remain in living contact with
Him: "I am the true vine and My Father is the vinedresser
... He who abides in Me, and I in him, bears much fruit;
for without Me you can do nothing" (vv. 1, 5). If a believer
does not maintain constant fellowship with Christ, he will
be fruitless—like a branch the gardener has cut off and
destroyed. Remaining connected to Christ, however, results in fruitfulness and effective prayer: "If you abide in
Me, and My words abide in you, you will ask what you
desire, and it shall be done for you" (v. 7). The result will
be spiritual joy: "These things I have spoken to you, that
My joy may remain in you, and that your joy may be full"
(v. 11); and fruit that is eternal: "You did not choose Me,
but I chose you and appointed you that you should go and
bear fruit, and that your fruit should remain" (v. 16).

Christ's divine plan for the Church is that He remain at
the center as the source of life and that individual believers be constantly connected to Him, drawing from Him the
nutrients they need to make the Church as a whole vigor-
ous and fruitful.

Christ is the cornerstone.

Old Testament prophecies concerning the Messiah oc-
casionally present Him as a stone. For example, God told
Moses to "strike the rock" and from it flowed the water the
Israelites needed to sustain life (Ex. 17:6). This reference
to living waters is typical of references to Christ. In
addition, the angel of the Lord revealed to the prophet
Zechariah that Christ would be the capstone of the temple
(Zech. 4:7). And God revealed to Isaiah that Christ would

be a "stone of stumbling and a rock of offense" to Israel
(Isa. 8:14).

Most significantly, the Old Testament makes clear that
Christ would be the cornerstone of His church. Psalm
118:22 refers to Him as a stone "the builders rejected" that
"has become the chief cornerstone." Isaiah 28:16 reveals
that God called the Messiah "a stone for a foundation, a
tried stone, a precious cornerstone, a sure foundation."
And Genesis 49 is the record of Jacob calling together his
sons to tell them what would happen "in the last days" (v.
1) and telling them that from Joseph would come "the
Shepherd, the Stone of Israel" (v. 24).

Christ told Peter He would build His church (Matt.
16:18) and implied the building would be ongoing. In his
letter to the Ephesians, Paul declared Jesus is the cornerstone of the Church and the apostles and prophets its
foundation (Eph. 2:19–22). Peter described the Church as
a spiritual house built of living stones—the true believers—with Christ as the cornerstone as Isaiah prophesied
(1 Peter 2:5–6). Paul spoke of Christ as the foundation of
the Church and those who believe in Him as God's temple,
and he reminds all believers that it is impossible to build
a Christian life apart from Christ (1 Cor. 3:11–17).

By its nature a stone is lifeless, but in His resurrection
Christ became the living stone. Believers who trust in
Him receive eternal life and become living stones with
which He builds His Church.

Christ is the high priest.

Christ fulfills the role of high priest, typified by Aaron
and Melchizedek, in offering himself as a sacrifice (Heb.
9:11–12), living eternally to intercede for us (Heb. 7:25),
and giving gifts to His Church (Rom. 8:32).

Believers in Christ also fulfill a priest's function by
offering their bodies as living sacrifices (Rom. 12:1), prais-
ing God with "the fruit of our lips," doing good works, and
sharing—"for with such sacrifices God is pleased" (Heb.
13:15–16). Coupled with the ministry of sacrifice is the
ministry of intercession as the believer-priest exercises his

privilege in prayer through Jesus Christ (Rom. 8:26–27;
Col. 4:12; 1 Tim. 2:1; Heb. 10:19–22). The truth of the
Church as a royal priesthood is one of the great doctrines
recovered in the Protestant Reformation and relates to
prayer and the believer's fellowship with God.

In the history of the Church, no one has doubted the fact
of Christ's priesthood, but some authorities question when
this priesthood began. Some scholars, however, have
traced it only to His glorification in heaven. Obviously, He
was functioning as a priest on earth, as He interceded for
His disciples and offered Himself as a sacrifice on the
cross. The best conclusion is that, in the beginning of
creation, God appointed Christ as a priest eternally, even
though Christ did not function in all aspects of this role
until His incarnation. Psalm 110:4 (see also Heb. 7:20–
21) declared Him a priest at least a thousand years before
His incarnation:

> The LORD has sworn
> And will not relent,
> "You are a priest forever
> According to the order of Melchizedek."

The continuous nature of His priesthood is also unique:
It cannot be changed and no successor is required. According to Hebrews 7:24, "But He, because He continues forever, has an unchangeable priesthood." Since Christ rose
from the dead, He is "able to save completely those who
come to God through Him, because He always lives to
intercede for them" (Heb. 7:25 NIV).

While Christ's priesthood is permanent, like
Melchizedek's, Christ also fulfills all the functions of the
Aaronic priesthood. In addition, Christ's service is supe-
rior to Aaron's because Christ's priesthood does not depend on lineage or require a successor. Christ also
ministers as a priest in heaven, interceding for believers,
a priestly function Aaron could perform only on earth.
Christ's sacrifice superseded Aaron's, who had to offer
sacrifice continually. Because Christ's sacrifice was final
and complete, He had to offer His sacrifice only once.

The Roman Catholic concept of Christ's sacrifice is that it is a perpetual offering and He must keep on sacrificing in order to continue His priesthood. The Protestant concept is that Christ died once with perpetual results. Christ's dying on the cross fulfilled all that redemption requires. He paid the price and redeemed mankind from the penalty of sin. In this propitiation, He satisfied all God's righteous demands for sacrifice. The result is that Christ provided complete reconciliation for man.

The Bible is clear that Christ died once for all. He does not need to offer up sacrifices daily, as Aaron and Melchizedek did, first for His own sins and then for the people's. This He did "once for all when He offered up Himself" (Heb. 7:27). The blood shed on the cross completed the sacrifice, and Christ entered heaven—the Holy Place—*through* the blood, but not *with* the blood (Heb. 9:12; 13:12 NIV). Having completed the sacrifice and having purged our sins, He "sat down at the right hand of the Majesty on high" (Heb. 1:3).

On the basis of His sacrifice, Christ is able to intercede for the saints in heaven and, sitting at the right hand of the Father, He is able to intercede for us as well: "Who is he who condemns? It is Christ who died, and furthermore is also risen, who is even at the right hand of God, who also makes intercession for us" (Rom. 8:34; Heb. 7:25).

The doctrine of Christ's work as a priest assures believers of their salvation and of Christ's intercession on their behalf in heaven.

Christ is the head of the church.

Ephesians 4:15–16 describes the Church as an organism with individual members growing and developing. Those members differ in their characteristics and gifts, yet unite to fulfill a common unified function (Rom. 12:3–8; 1 Cor. 12:4–28; Eph. 4:4, 11–16). The body of Christ, although diverse in its members and gifts, is one body (Eph. 1:23; 2:15–16; 3:6; 4:12–16; 5:30; Col. 1:24; 2:19). The figure of Christ as the head and the Church as His body is rich in spiritual truth and sets apart the Church as a distinct entity in God's divine plan.

Prior to the Day of Pentecost, the concept of the body was not used to describe the relationship of believers to God. According to 1 Corinthians 12:12–14, the baptism of the Spirit is what forms the body of Christ:

> For as the body is one and has many members, but all the members of that one body, being many, are one body, so also is Christ. For by one Spirit we were all baptized into one body—whether Jews or Greeks, whether slaves or free—and have all been made to drink into one Spirit. For in fact the body is not one member but many.

God the Father appointed Christ as head of the church: "And He put all things under His feet, and gave Him to be head over all things to the church, which is His body, the fullness of Him who fills all in all" (Eph. 1:22–23). Scripture makes clear that as joints and sinews join the physical body, so parts of the Church body connect and create a living, growing organism (Col. 2:19).

As head of the body, Christ directs the Church which is His bride (Eph. 5:23). Christ is not an arbitrary or unreasonable Lord over the church. Rather, like the head of a physical body, He directs His body and determines what is good for it as well as what will accomplish God's will. The important point is that in the constant relationship of life, a living connection to the head causes the body to function properly.

Each member of the body has certain gifts and abilities, as outlined in Romans 12:3–8; 1 Corinthians 12:27–28; and Ephesians 4:7–16. In the early church some were apostles, some prophets, and some evangelists. Some of their gifts were temporary; others were permanent gifts to the Church and continue to operate today. All come together to fulfill God's will for His Son's work.

Christ is the new Adam.

The first man, Adam, plunged mankind into sin and death. His act served to separate mankind into segments, such as Jew and Gentile, and to cause each succeeding generation throughout time to inherit a sinful nature, as well as to suffer the lasting effects of the sins of the generations who preceded them.

Christ, who is sinless, created new life that is available to all who believe in Him:

> Therefore, if anyone is in Christ, he is a new creation; old things have passed away; behold, all things have become new. (2 Cor. 5:17)

> For He Himself is our peace, who has made both one . . . having abolished in His flesh . . . the law of commandments contained in ordinances, so as to create in Himself one new man from the two. (Eph. 2:14–16)

> Put on the new man which was created according to God, in righteousness and true holiness. (Eph. 4:24)

In the new creation, Jew and Gentile are one humanity, equal in privilege, blessing, and grace: "There is neither Jew nor Greek . . . you are all one in Christ Jesus" (Gal. 3:28); "There is neither Greek nor Jew . . . but Christ is all and in all" (Col. 3:11); "[you are] a new creation" (Gal. 6:15).

The new humanity flows from the resurrected Christ—the new Adam, the new beginning.

Christ is the bridegroom.

The role of Christ as the bridegroom and the Church the bride predicts the glorious future of the Church at the close of the age. It speaks of Christ's infinite love manifested in His sacrifice, His present intercession, and His blessing on His future bride.

Paul spoke of the spiritual church as a chaste virgin in 2 Corinthians 11:2 and stated a betrothal had taken place. In Ephesians 5:26 he indicated that Christ will sanctify and cleanse the Church, making it "a glorious church, not having spot or wrinkle or any such thing, but that it should be holy and without blemish" (5:27).

Understanding the significance of these descriptions requires some understanding of the marriage customs of Paul's time. First, the parents of the bride and groom reached a legal agreement for the couple to marry. This agreement began the betrothal period, and although a wedding would not take place until later, once the agreement was made, the couple were legally committed to each other. Because the betrothal was binding, neither person could be released from the commitment without a divorce. Next, at the appointed time, usually a year later, the bridegroom would come for his bride and the wedding would take place. Then, the couple would celebrate the marriage at the wedding feast.

These ancient customs relate directly to the prophecy and the future of the spiritual church. In the present age the Church is betrothed to Christ—totally committed, having been bought by His blood. Christ will come for His bride and meet her in the air: "For the Lord Himself will descend from heaven with a shout, with the voice of an archangel, and with the trumpet of God. And the dead in Christ will rise first. Then we who are alive and remain shall be caught up together with them in the clouds to meet the Lord in the air. And thus we shall always be with the Lord" (1 Thess. 4:16–17).

The wedding feast is described in Revelation 19:7–9. Some believe the feast will take place in heaven; others anticipate it will occur at the beginning of the millennium. As the wedding feast is described in Revelation 19:7–9 in connection with the millennium, it may take place after the Second Coming.

The Destiny of the Church

The prophetic future of the church outlined in Scripture includes the rapture and transformation of the church; the judgment seat of Christ; the church reigning with Christ in the millennium; and the church sharing in the blessings of the new Jerusalem and eternal state (see chapter 14).

Apart from indicating that the church will reign with Christ and will serve Him, the Bible does not reveal much detail of the activities of the church in eternity. Undoubtedly its main occupation will be to worship God along with the saints of all ages. The transcending fact is that all the saints will be "with Christ" and in His Presence forever. Because God does all things well the experiences He has planned for us in heaven will be all that our hearts could wish. Friends and loved ones will be together forever and earth's sorrows and problems will be no more. As Paul said, to be with Christ will be "far better" (Phil. 1:23) than any situation on earth could possibly be. Our struggles with sinful, deteriorating bodies will be past. In our new bodies we will have abounding health and strength. Heaven will be the ultimate paradise and no one will be able to find any room for improvement, for if a better eternity could be created, God would create it. The wonderful truth is that paradise could be ours momentarily for the Rapture may occur soon.

— 8 —

THE EIGHTH KEY

The Intermediate State

Throughout time mankind has been concerned with what will happen to their souls when their bodies die. Consequently, a number of theories have developed that are not Bible-based and, therefore, are false.

All life ceases with physical death

Atheism and some Far Eastern religions deny God's existence. Therefore, atheists believe life ends when the physical body dies. According to this theory, man is simply an intelligent animal without moral purpose or divine intent. The Brahman and Buddhist concepts of nirvana are somewhat similar. These religions teach that man has no material existence after death and his being is absorbed by a supreme spirit.

Conditional morality

Some liberal theologians suggest that life after death is conditional and depends on the worthiness of an individual's earthly life. Consequently, they teach that those who are judged unworthy of life after death will simply never be resurrected. This concept permits the dismissal of all thoughts of eternal punishment and suggests a partial annihilation of the human race. The conclusion is that only those God considers "good" will live after death.

Universalism

Other liberal theologians suggest that in the end all men will be saved. They find support for this theory in the fact that God loves all mankind. They believe that universal love guarantees all persons will ultimately be forgiven and receive salvation. Some also say that, since Christ died for the world, the entire world is saved. These theories disregard the many scriptures contradicting universalism, including those that reveal God's righteous character and His judgment of the wicked.

Restitutionalism

A variation of universalism, restitutionalism is based on a misunderstanding of texts that speak of the restoration of all saints, such as Acts 3:21. This theory suggests the wicked will receive some punishment, but in the end both wicked angels and wicked men will be saved.

Transmigration

Various non-Christian religions believe that at death a man's soul passes into another body. While affirming that physical death is not the cessation of existence, this belief suggests man does not necessarily continue as a man. Transmigration of the human soul might result in an individual existing in animal form. This possibility sometimes leads to the idea that animals should not be killed for any reason.

Purgatory

The teaching that at death men pass into a state of suffering in order to be purged of sin is a prominent feature of Roman Catholic eschatology. This doctrine teaches that many prayers of intercession must be offered before the souls of the dead will be released. It seems to suggest that the amount of time an individual's soul must spend in purgatory paying for sins committed during his lifetime is dependent on the severity of his sins, as well as on the concern his friends and family continue to have for him after his physical death. The theory of purgatory encourages individuals to make contributions to the church to beg priests to offer prayers for the dead. To a degree this practice would seem to tie an individual's time in purgatory to the wealth of his survivors.

Protestant theology rejects the concept of purgatory. It is contradicted by the fact that the believer is cleansed and forgiven all sin at the moment of salvation and is justified by faith in Jesus Christ.

The Doctrine of the Intermediate State

Sheol is the word used in the Old Testament to describe the grave where the body is placed as well as the conscious state of existence of a soul after physical death. According to a number of passages (2 Sam. 22:6; Ps. 18:5, for example), the souls of the righteous and the unrighteous go to Sheol, indicating it is a place of conscious existence and has two compartments. Psalm 116:3 describes Sheol as a place of sorrow: "The pains of death surrounded me, / And the pangs of Sheol laid hold of me; / I found trouble and sorrow." Jonah speaks of calling to the Lord from Sheol (Jonah 2:2), and Ezekiel records the Lord revealed to him that the dead speak "out of the midst of hell" (Ezek. 32:21).

The NIV translates most usages of this word as references to the grave. Apparently the translators were opposed to the idea that Sheol could have two compartments. However, indications are that it does, because the term is used to describe the experience of both the righteous and the unrighteous in the Old Testament. The theory of two compartments suggests one is for the wicked who are in conscious suffering, and the other is for the righteous whom God blesses. Some authorities suggest that when used in relation to the righteous, Sheol refers only to the grave. Most conservative interpreters favor the concept of two compartments for Sheol.

The Old Testament does not offer believers joyous hope and confidence of bliss for life after death with the same clarity as the New Testament, where additional revelation is given.

The New Testament Doctrine of the Intermediate State

In the New Testament the word *Hades* serves as a synonym for Sheol. A central passage concerning this

doctrine of the intermediate state is Luke 16:19–31.
Lazarus, the poor beggar whom Jesus resurrected, lay in
the bosom of Abraham, while the rich man suffered the
torment of fire. Both were alive and conscious, had mem-
ories of their former lives, and although a great division
was between them, were even able to communicate with
each other. Taken literally, this passage confirms the
two-compartment concept of Sheol/Hades.

Many believe a change took place at Christ's resurrection and that now the righteous go immediately to the
presence of God in heaven, while only the unsaved remain
in Hades. This change is indicated by Ephesians 4:8–10,
which describes Christ leading a multitude of captives into
heaven when he ascended, and His words to the criminal
crucified with Him, "Assuredly, I say to you, today you will
be with Me in Paradise" (Luke 23:43).

Second Corinthians 5:8 promises that now the righteous
who die are immediately "present with the Lord," and
Revelation 6:9–11 and 7:9–17 describe the martyred dead
in heaven. Whatever theory may be adopted regarding
the character of Sheol and Hades prior to Christ's resurrection, it is clear that now, because of His resurrection,
the righteous are in heaven and only the wicked remain
in hell.

Scripture does not support the theory that the soul
sleeps in the body in the grave until resurrection. Paul
regarded departing from this life equivalent to being with
Christ (2 Cor. 5:8; Phil. 1:23). While the body may be
"sleeping," the soul is in conscious existence in the presence of God in heaven.

Interpreters differ as to whether the saints of old received temporary bodies immediately after death while
remaining in the intermediate state, or whether they
remain disembodied. However, the description of the rich
man and Lazarus in Luke 16 describes both of them
having bodies. According to 2 Corinthians 5:1–5, if our
earthly houses are dissolved, we are given houses in
heaven. And Revelation 6:9–11 describes the martyred

dead standing before God, and receiving white robes.
These descriptions seem to require bodies.

All agree that an intermediate body, like the intermediate state, is temporary and will be replaced by an eternal
body. The prophecies apply to both the saved and the
unsaved, for the eternal order will not be fully established
until all have been resurrected, judged, and given their
eternal rewards. The saved will receive their resurrection
bodies in a series of resurrections that begin with the
Rapture of the church and continue with the later resurrection of other saints at the Second Coming. The unsaved
will not be raised until the end of the millennium.

— 9 —

THE NINTH KEY

The Rapture

On the night before Jesus' crucifixion, the disciples were greatly concerned when He said He was about to leave them. Peter asked, "Where are You going, Lord?" and Christ replied, "Where I am going you cannot follow Me now, but you shall follow Me afterward" (John 13:36). Then Christ told the disciples not to worry, for He would return and take them to heaven. He said, "Let not your heart be troubled; you believe in God, believe also in Me. In My Father's house are many mansions; if it were not so, I would have told you. I go to prepare a place for you. And . . . I will come again and receive you to Myself; that where I am, there you may be also" (John 14:1–3).

This promise was the first mention of the Rapture, and because it is not mentioned anywhere in the Old Testament, the concept was totally new to the disciples. They still expected Christ to establish an earthly kingdom during their lifetimes and then to rescue the nation of Israel from her persecutors and give each disciple a prominent role in judging the twelve tribes (Matt. 19:28–30). They had not come to a full understanding of Christ's statements that revealed He would return to heaven and later would come to earth again when He would establish His kingdom. To the degree the disciples understood Christ would come a second time, they believed the fulfillment of this new promise to "receive you to Myself" was a part of the promise to come to earth a second time.

Much later Paul was converted, and God revealed the doctrine of the Rapture to him. Paul began to incorporate those details into his teaching for new converts. Acts 17:1 – 3 records the details of a short visit Paul made to Thessalonica where he preached the Gospel in the temple on three Sabbath days. Apparently he introduced the doctrine of the Rapture to the Thessalonians, for later they posed theological questions about it. Consequently, when Paul wrote his two letters to them, he explained the Rapture at length.

To a degree, the Thessalonian Christians understood Paul's teaching and embraced the idea that Christ would return to take them to heaven. They also understood He could return at anytime. However, since Paul's departure, some of their number had died. The people were concerned about when they would see their loved ones again. They wondered if when Christ returned for the living He would also take with Him the Christians who had died.

Accordingly, in the first letter, Paul spoke to the people as believers who "wait for His Son from heaven" (1 Thess. 1:10). "What is our hope, or joy, or crown of rejoicing?" he asked. "Is it not even you in the presence of our Lord Jesus Christ at His coming?" (2:19). He assured them they would be "blameless in holiness before our God and Father at the coming of our Lord Jesus Christ with all His saints" (3:13).

Paul wanted the Thessalonians to understand this doctrine. He said he did not want them to be ignorant about God's future plans because they might grieve as those "who have no hope" do (4:13).

The certainty of the Rapture is made clear in verse 14 by the fundamental truth that Christ died and rose again. Paul did not say the Rapture is equally important to Christ's resurrection, but that it is equally certain. Because the people believed in the death and resurrection of Christ, which once was prophecy but at that time had become history, they could be certain that "even so God will bring with Him those who sleep in Jesus."

According to this passage, when the rapture of the church occurs Jesus will bring the souls in heaven with Him to be resurrected:

> For this we say to you by the word of the Lord, that we who are alive and remain until the coming of the Lord will by no means precede those who are asleep. For the Lord himself will descend from heaven with a shout, with the voice of an archangel, and with the trumpet of God. And the dead in Christ will rise first. Then we who are alive and remain shall be caught up together with them in the clouds to meet the Lord in the air. And thus we shall always be with the Lord.   (4:15–17)

Paul describes the scene as the Lord coming bodily from heaven to the air above the earth and issuing a loud command, accompanied by the voice of Michael, the Archangel. A trumpet call from God will be the signal for Christians who have died to be resurrected. A moment later Christians still living will also be "caught up," or raptured, with those who are resurrected to meet the Lord in the air. This rapturing is described as being "in the clouds," a reference either to atmospheric clouds or to the multitude of those being raised in the sense of "so great a cloud of witnesses" (Heb. 12:1). Once they meet the Lord in the air they go to heaven in fulfillment of the prophecy of going to the Father's house (John 14:2–3). Paul exhorted the Thessalonians to encourage and comfort one another with this promise.

First Corinthians 15 reveals more about the Rapture, saying that the human bodies of both those who have died and those who are living will be transformed instantly into bodies suited for heaven (vv. 51–52). This passage makes clear that our present bodies are not suited for heaven because they are perishable, or subject to decay (v. 53), and afflicted with mortality. A further difficulty is that our present bodies are sinful and need to be transformed into bodies like Christ's (Phil. 3:21). Those who died and went to heaven left their bodies behind and will not be complete until they receive their resurrection bodies.

The Rapture Contrasted to the
Second Coming

In the history of the Church there has been controversy over when the Rapture will take place. Many Bible scholars seem to interpret Scripture as saying the Rapture is a phase of the Second Coming. This belief is in keeping with the amillennial view that the millennium is not literal and, therefore, the details of the Rapture can be merged with those describing the Second Coming. The postmillennial view also does not recognize the Rapture as a separate event.

Those who are premillennial, however, generally regard the Rapture as a distinct event occurring some years before the second coming of Christ. Although the controversy has not been settled on the basis of many Scripture passages, it is an important, practical question. The correct answer indicates whether believers should expect Christ to come for His Church momentarily, or if many years must elapse and many events take place before this event can happen.

The Timing of the Rapture

No biblical passage states precisely when the Rapture will occur in relation to the tribulation or the Second Coming. However, major prophecies point to the conclusion that only a rapture preceding the tribulation would be a literal fulfillment of Scripture.

First, the Rapture is a movement from earth to heaven, whereas the Second Coming is a movement from heaven to earth. Therefore, the Rapture is completely separate from the Second Coming.

Second, the doctrine of the rapture is a simple one. Prophecies make no mention of angels or attending hosts, and no mention of judgment on earth to follow. The Rapture's single purpose is to take the Church from earth to heaven. The Second Coming will be a very complicated event. Instead of being a momentary act of God, as apparently the Rapture will be, the Second Coming will take

place over many hours as a gigantic procession of millions
of saints and angels move from heaven to earth, as Revelation 19:11–16 describes. It would be impossible to describe two events more distinct from each other than the
Rapture and the Second Coming.

Finally, in all passages concerning the Rapture, a preceding event is never mentioned. But those passages that
describe the Second Coming prophesy many events occurring first. Christ's description of His second coming is
recorded in Matthew 24, and chapters 6 through 18 of
Revelation provide many details. Accordingly, while
Scripture uniformly presents the Rapture as imminent,
the Second Coming is by no means imminent if the prophecies of events described as preceding it are to be literally
fulfilled.

The posttribulational view of the Rapture usually con-
sists of arguments against the pretribulation theory, but
proponents of the posttribulation view seldom offer any
substantial evidence to support their belief. In the history
of eschatology, posttribulationists have experienced major
divisions among themselves, because many of their beliefs
are not borne out by Scripture.

Until World War II, most posttribulationists argued
that the Tribulation, like the Rapture, was not a literal
prophecy. In fact, many held that the Tribulation was
simply an allegorical presentation of the sufferings of
saints in all ages and not intended to be literally fulfilled.
With the development and availability of the atomic bomb
during World War II, the possibility of millions of people
being destroyed encouraged most posttribulationists to
adopt a more realistic view. They came to recognize that
the Second Coming must be preceded by a time of tremendous trouble, which is specifically described in various
passages. Therefore, because these events have not occurred, the Second Coming is not imminent. Even so,
posttribulationists tend to try to prove that Christians will
endure the tribulation with relative ease.

An examination of the nature of God's judgments, however, reveals that if Christians were present during the tribulation they would not escape the trouble, because judgments are against an entire civilization. The judgments prophesied for this period include pestilence, stars falling from heaven, war, and famine. Events of those kinds do not single out non-Christians to suffer the effects of such devastation, while Christians are spared. All living people, regardless of who they are, would have to endure the catastrophes. Furthermore, Revelation 12 reveals God will cast Satan—described as a dragon—out of heaven. Consequently, Satan would have great wrath against God's people (Rev. 12:12–17). Christians would not only be exposed to the worldwide catastrophes, but would also be subjected to Satan's anger, as well as the world ruler's who will attempt to put to death all who do not worship him (Rev. 13:7, 15).

Therefore, any realistic view of the future time, which Christ referred to as the Great Tribulation, includes the realization that a rapture climaxing the tribulation is hardly a blessed hope. A doctrine that teaches otherwise does not fit with Christ's command to "let not your hearts be troubled" (John 14:1), Paul's exhortation to comfort and encourage (1 Thess. 4:18), or the concept of the Rapture being a "blessed hope" (Titus 2:13). The Thessalonians who were grieving for their loved ones would hardly have been comforted if they had been told they had to go through an extended period of suffering, during which most of them would be killed, before the Rapture would occur. No such warning regarding the Rapture can be found in Scripture.

Paul's discussion of the Day of the Lord in 1 Thessalonians 5 supports the concept of a pretribulation rapture. Both pre- and posttribulationists agree the Day of the Lord follows the Rapture. In fact, they agree the Day of the Lord begins when the Rapture occurs (1 Thess. 5:1).

The "Day of the Lord" is an expression frequently used in both the Old and New Testaments to describe any

period of time during which God exercises direct judgment
on human sin. The Old Testament records a number of
times when Israel endured a day of the Lord, lasting a few
days or, in some cases, several years. Prophecy of the
future Day of the Lord describes a lengthy period, extending for the entire time of the millennial kingdom, when
God will judge all mankind. As Paul made clear in 1
Thessalonians 5, the Day of the Lord begins with the
Rapture.

After Paul wrote 1 Thessalonians, teachers went to the
Thessalonian church and tried to connect their own suffering and persecution with prophecies of the Day of the
Lord. They told the people at Thessalonica the Day of the
Lord had begun. When Paul heard of these misrepresen-
tations, he wrote a second letter, pointing out that the
visiting teachers were wrong:

> Now, brethren, concerning the coming of our Lord Jesus
> Christ and our gathering together to Him, we ask you, not
> to be soon shaken in mind or troubled, either by spirit or
> by word or by letter, as if from us, as though the day of
> Christ had come. Let no one deceive you by any means; for
> that Day will not come unless the falling away comes first,
> and the man of sin is revealed, the son of perdition, who
> opposes and exalts himself above all that is called God or
> that is worshiped, so that he sits as God in the temple of
> God, showing himself that he is God.   (2 Thess. 2:1–4)

The warning not to be deceived (v. 3) by those who
preach and teach falsely still applies. The insight Paul
gives for the sequence of events surrounding the end time
reveals the events will take place in a specific order. When
compared to other revelations, particularly Christ's description recorded in Matthew 24, we know the Second
Coming will occur after the period of the Great Tribulation—the Day of the Lord, and the Rapture will occur as
it begins. Notice these facts:

- The "falling away" will occur before the Second Coming (2 Thess. 2:3).
- The "man of sin" must come to power and reveal
  himself before the Second Coming will occur (v. 3).

- The "mystery of lawlessness" is already at work but "He who now restrains" will continue to restrain until the "lawless one" is destroyed at the Second Coming (vv. 7–8).

The Rapture must occur before these end-time events.

If we believe divine inspiration was the source of Paul's understanding of these events, then the only possible conclusion is that the Great Tribulation will begin and extend for some period of time before the Second Coming will occur. The same arguments also prove the Rapture will occur before the Great Tribulation.

The foundational principles of eschatology are revealed by Jesus Christ, the Son of God. During His thirty-three-year lifetime, He was God on earth. The Bible as God's word infallibly records these truths. As recorded in Matthew 24:15–31, Christ described the events that will precede the Second Coming and will occur after the Rapture. In this passage Christ does not discuss the Rapture itself, but those events that will follow it. His description of the Second Coming contains no reference to the rapture of the Church.

According to Scripture, in the end time the Roman Empire will be revived. Ten nations will band together to form a confederacy. This will be a major event (Dan. 7:7–8, 23–24). When this ten-nation group achieves political power, a dictator will arise who will conquer three of the countries and then the remaining seven (Dan. 7:8, 24). The resulting power will support the world dictatorship in control during the last three and a half years before the Second Coming.

Once the man of sin has established his control of the ten nations, he will impose a peace treaty on Israel. As stated in Daniel 9:27, the man of sin is the prince who will come, who will make this covenant with Israel, and the covenant will be in effect for seven years. When these events occur, the informed Bible student will recognize the man in power as the one prophesied to appear at the beginning of the Day of the Lord (2 Thess. 2:3). Since the man in power's appearance predates the Second Coming by more than seven years, it is clear that the Rapture will occur more than seven years before the Second Coming.

If the Rapture were to occur simultaneously with the Second Coming, the martyred dead of the tribulation would not require a special resurrection (Rev. 20:4–6), which will likely occur several days after the Second Coming.

Matthew 25:31–48 describes a judgment falling on the Gentiles living at the Second Coming. The passage indicates that Christ will set up His throne on earth some time after the Second Coming (v. 31). This passage describes the Gentiles intermingled as sheep and goats, indicating both saved and unsaved are still on the earth together. If a rapture had taken place some time before, a separation would have taken place while Christ was still in the air. The fact that there is no mention of separation is additional proof there will be no rapture at the time of the Second Coming.

Other Scriptural evidence that the two events are quite different gives sufficient basis for those who believe in a pretribulation rapture to expect Christ to come for His church at any time, without warning.

Many of the same arguments that support a pretribulation rapture also prove improbable the concept that Christ will come in the middle of the last seven years. This belief is the mid-tribulation view. (For a more detailed discussion of this subject, see the author's book, entitled *The Rapture Question.*)

Events Subsequent to the Rapture

As the Rapture is the first in a sequence of events, Scripture gives an outline of what the church can expect in the future. Following the meeting of the Lord in the air, the Church will appear at the judgment seat of Christ to receive her reward (2 Cor. 5:10–11). The Church will return with Christ to the earth at His Second Coming and will reign with Him. Following the completion of the millennial kingdom, the Church will share with the saints of other ages the blessings of dwelling in the new Jerusalem in the new heaven and the new earth (see chapter 14).

10

THE TENTH KEY

The Great Tribulation

The organized church has tended to ignore scriptural revelation of the specifics of the Great Tribulation. Modern liberals claim that a loving God would not harshly judge mankind, even though Scripture is very clear that God's righteousness demands judgment. Even evangelicals who accept the Bible as the inspired Word of God tend to neglect the passages dealing with the Great Tribulation. Many of them try to explain away the time of great distress as something that occurred in the troubles of the early church.

Tribulation characterizes the human race. A careful study of Scripture reveals there have been many times of trouble in the past, and those periods have included judgment. Scripture also reveals there will be a future time of three and a half years of unprecedented trouble immediately preceding Christ's second coming. The details of this period are an important feature of prophecy, particularly in that they indicate the church will be removed from earth before the beginning of this period and will not experience God's wrath.

Early Scriptures predict that Israel and the world will be judged. As recorded in Deuteronomy 28, Moses warned the children of Israel that God would curse them and scatter them all over the world and that they would face constant trouble. This tribulation will climax in the period just before Christ's second coming when Israel will be under special persecution.

Jeremiah predicted the Babylonian captivity, and his prediction was fulfilled during his lifetime. He also predicted the future trials of Israel that will occur in the end time. Jeremiah and other prophets foretold the regathering of Israel when the people will be returned to their ancient land. However, before they are delivered completely from God's judgment that scattered them, they will experience an awful time of tribulation:

> For thus says the LORD:
> "We have heard a voice of trembling,
> Of fear, and not of peace.
> Ask now, and see,
> Whether a man is ever in labor with child?
> So why do I see every man with his hands on his loins
> Like a woman in labor,
> And all faces turned pale?
> Alas! For that day is great,
> So that none is like it.
> And it is the time of Jacob's trouble,
> But he shall be saved out of it."   (Jer. 30:5–7)

The tribulation will end when the nation Israel is regathered:

> "For it shall come to pass in that day,"
> Says the LORD of hosts,
> "That I will break his yoke from your neck,
> And will burst your bonds;
> Foreigners shall no more enslave them.
> But they shall serve the LORD their God,
> And David their king,
> Whom I will raise up for them."   (vv. 8–9)

David will be resurrected at the Second Coming, which will be the beginning of Christ's kingdom on earth which is predicted throughout the Old and New Testaments:

> "For I am with you," says the LORD, "to save you;
> Though I make a full end of all nations where I have
>   scattered you,
> Yet I will not make a complete end of you.
> But I will correct you in justice,
> And will not let you go altogether unpunished."   (v. 11)

The book of Joel specifically describes a day of the Lord—a time of trouble that Israel would experience. The Old Testament also describes other days of the Lord when the Lord would directly judge Israel. Some of these prophecies have already been fulfilled. For example, several of Joel's prophecies concern the Assyrian invasion, which has already occurred. But a careful study of these prophecies reveals that they go far beyond what happened when Assyria invaded Israel. The ultimate fulfillment will be the day of the Lord that will occur at the Second Coming:

I will show wonders in the heavens and in the earth:
Blood and fire and pillars of smoke.
The sun shall be turned into darkness,
And the moon into blood,
Before the coming of the great and terrible day of the
    LORD.
And it shall come to pass
That whoever calls on the name of the LORD
Shall be saved.
For in Mount Zion and in Jerusalem there shall be
    deliverance,
As the LORD has said,
Among the remnant whom the LORD calls.   (Joel 2:30–32)

Israel's final restoration ultimately involves their being regathered from all over the world, as many Old Testament Scriptures reveal (Jer. 30:10–11; 31:10–14; Ezek. 39:25–29; Amos 9:11–15).

The World Ruler

The Great Tribulation is the final chapter of world history and leads directly to the Second Coming. This period will be preceded by the rapture of the church and the reemergence of the Roman Empire.

Daniel 7:7 predicts the revived Roman Empire will be the last form of the fourth great kingdom to follow Babylon. Verse 24 indicates the ten horns of the beast mentioned in the seventh verse describe ten kings. Although they are first presented symbolically as horns, there is no

question that the ten kings are ten rulers who will be
involved with the final stage of the Roman Empire.

Old Testament prophecies characteristically skip the
present age. Many Scriptures, particularly those dealing
with the first and second comings of Christ, do not specifically discuss a time period between Christ's birth, death,
and resurrection and His earthly kingdom. In fact, during
Christ's earthly ministry apparently no one understood
that there would be a first and a second coming of Christ
with a time interval between. Not until Christ ascended
to heaven did the disciples realize that He had fulfilled the
prophecies of His suffering and death but not those of His
glorious reign or that fulfillment of these prophecies would
require a second coming.

Today there is similar confusion about the Rapture and
the Second Coming because many believers fail to recognize there will be a period of time between these events.
However, others understand there will be an interval of
time, because the Rapture is very different from the Second Coming. The Rapture is a movement from earth to
heaven, whereas the Second Coming is a movement from
heaven to earth that will take place in an entirely different
set of circumstances. In the same manner, Old Testament
prophecies skip the period of the decline of the Roman
Empire, discussing only the future events that will immediately precede the Second Coming when the revived
Roman Empire will emerge.

According to Daniel 7:8, there will be an eleventh horn,
a ruler who will first conquer three of the ten kings and
then, apparently, the other seven: "I was considering the
horns, and there was another horn, a little one, coming up
among them, before whom three of the first horns were
plucked out by the roots. And there, in this horn, were
eyes like the eyes of a man, and a mouth speaking pompous
words." This ruler's political power will eventually be that
of a kingdom that encompasses the whole world: "[It] shall
be different from all other kingdoms, / And shall devour
the whole earth" (v. 23).

Once this ruler gets control of all ten countries, he will
be the political strong man in the Middle East and will
impose a peace treaty on Israel as predicted in Daniel 9:27.
While Scripture does not record the details, apparently
this treaty will include establishing Israel's borders and
will direct the relationships with the countries surrounding Israel. Israel will bask under the protection of this
ruler and the nation will be able to relax her present-day
military protection.

This "little horn" of Daniel 7:8 is "the prince who is to
come" mentioned in Daniel 9:26. He is also the king
described by Daniel 11:36 who will declare himself God
and will eventually rule over the world. This world ruler
is the "man of sin" referred to by 2 Thessalonians 2:3–4.
He is sometimes referred to as "the antichrist." Although
Scripture does not assign this title to him, it is found in 1
John 2:18; 4:3; and 2 John 1:7. In Revelation 13, this world
government is described as the beast "out of the sea," (v.
1). The ruler is revealed in verses 3 and 4 that describe
one of the heads of the beast being "mortally wounded, and
his deadly wound was healed. And all the world marveled
and followed the beast."

This man will be Satan's masterpiece, his king of kings
and lord of lords, his evil substitute for Jesus Christ. This
ruler will dominate the world during the last half of the
seven-year period immediately preceding the Second
Coming, as described in Daniel 9:27. As ruler of the ten
kings he will make the covenant with Israel and then
break it in the middle of the seven years, bringing "an end
to sacrifice and offering." The remaining three and a half
years of his rule, the precise period of the world government, will be one of "abominations," for he "shall be one
who makes desolate." The length of the second half of the
world ruler's reign is made clear by Revelation 13:5, which
specifically states that his rule will be extended for "forty-
two months." The nineteenth chapter of Revelation reveals that this ruler's reign will end at the second coming
of Christ.

The Covenant with Israel

This man, described as "the prince who is to come" in Daniel 9:26, will make a covenant with Israel. He will observe the covenant for the first half of the seven years and then break it. The covenant will bring peace to the Middle East and the whole world will honor it as a peace movement (Ezek. 38:8, 11, 14; 1 Thess. 5:3), but it will clearly be broken after three and a half years (Dan. 9:27; Matt. 24:15; Rev. 13:5). This three and a half year period immediately preceding the Second Coming is the Great Tribulation.

The Great War with Israel

According to Ezekiel 38—39, a nation described as the land to the far north of Israel—most likely Russia or another state of the former Soviet Union—(38:6, 15; 39:2)—assisted by other nations named in Ezekiel 38:5–6, will attack Israel, challenging the peace covenant made with the Middle East ruler. Although scholars differ as to when this will occur in end-time events, indications are that the war will begin in the period of peace following the Rapture. Of course, it will follow the making of the covenant with Israel. The war will be a disaster for the armies invading Israel because God will intervene and by supernatural means destroy the invaders (38:19–39:5). A great earthquake will hamper the invaders (38:19–20) and disorder in the invading army will confuse them so that they will fight each other (38:21). A great plague will cause much bloodshed, and rain, hailstones, and burning sulfur will come from the sky (38:22). By these acts of God, the army of the invaders will be completely destroyed: "You shall fall upon the mountains of Israel, you and all your troops and the peoples who are with you; I will give you to birds of prey of every sort and to the beasts of the field to be devoured" (39:4). (The King James translation of Ezekiel 39:2, indicating that "the sixth part of thee" will survive, is not an accurate translation.)

This battle will eliminate the power of the nations

formerly in the Soviet Union, as well as the other nations
who will join the attack on Israel. Their defeat will en-
hance the power of the Middle East ruler who will have
already conquered the ten kingdoms, and may be the
springboard that enables him to proclaim himself dictator
of the world.

The World Government

Until the twentieth century, the idea of a world government seemed virtually impossible to implement. Even
during the early years of this century when World War I
prompted attempts to organize the League of Nations, a
world government still seemed unlikely. The League of
Nations movement failed, but following World War II the
United Nations emerged. This body has grown in strength
and power and today is a weak form of world government
embracing most of the nations of the world.

Revelation 13:7 clearly states that the Middle Eastern
ruler will conquer the world. Apparently he will achieve
total control by proclamation. Daniel 7:23 which states he
"shall devour the whole earth," gives additional insight to
the meaning of the Revelation passage, which states, "It
was granted to him to make war with the saints and to
overcome them. And authority was given him over every
tribe, tongue, and nation."

Today all the necessary physical components that would
make a world government possible have emerged. Instant
communication around the globe, an absolute necessity for
a world government to maintain its power, is possible via
radio, telephone, television, and other twentieth century
technologies.

Rapid transportation is another necessity that is now
available. The dramatic difference between the speed of
transporting troops and supplies during the Gulf War in
early 1992 and during World War II, for example,
illustrates the capabilities of newer technological develop-
ments. During World War II ships carried men and supplies across the sea. During the Gulf War, however, huge

aircraft delivered troops and equipment to the Middle East within hours. Rapid deployment played a large part in the allied force's victorious conclusion of the war. Even fifty years ago, deploying such an army and providing supplies and equipment would have taken months. In the interim, Saddam Hussein could have consolidated his hold on the Middle East. Perhaps only a world war would have dislodged him.

Giant computers, which bind the world together with electronic data, also make a world government feasible. Before this kind of technology was developed, many people questioned the prophecy concerning the Great Tribulation found in Revelation 13:16–17. This passage states that the world ruler will require everyone to receive the "mark or the name of the beast" before buying or selling: "He causes all, both small and great, rich and poor, free and slave, to receive a mark on their right hand or on their foreheads, and that no one may buy or sell except one who has the mark or the name of the beast, or the number of his name."

To receive such a mark, the people would have to recognize the world ruler as God and Satan as the supreme deity. Thousands will refuse to do this, and, according to Revelation 20:4–6, they will be beheaded. They will be resurrected at the Second Coming to reign with Christ for a thousand years. There is no doubt that with today's technology, a world ruler, who is in total control, would have the ability to keep a continually updated census of all living persons and know day-by-day precisely which people had pledged their allegiance to him and received the mark and which had not.

The feasibility of a world government with today's technology is also supported by the fact that a destructive missile can be accurately delivered to anywhere in the world in thirty minutes. A ruler with total control of the world's missile warfare would have the ability to enforce whatever laws he might desire or almost instantly destroy large segments of population should some refuse to obey him.

These twentieth century inventions make a world government mechanically feasible. All these facts add up to the conclusion that the world stage is now set for the final drama. The events that will lead to the second coming of Christ are awaiting only the rapture of the church.

The Final Three and One-half Years

Because the world dictator will blaspheme against God and break his covenant with Israel, persecuting them as well as Christians and any others who refuse to worship him as God, the Great Tribulation will be a time of God's great judgments. This truth is revealed at length in both the Old and New Testaments, especially in Revelation 6–18. A survey of these chapters reveals there will be war, famine, pestilence, demon possession, stars falling from heaven, earthquakes, and a disruption of the ordinary course of nature. Even a casual study of Revelation reveals the awful catastrophes that will occur. The result of all these events will be that most of the world's population will be destroyed.

Throughout history the church has shown a tendency to disregard these prophecies as if they will not be literally fulfilled. While the language of certain passages in the book of Revelation, as well as other prophetic passages in the Bible, is symbolic, interspersed among the symbols are statements that must be interpreted literally as God's explanation of the meaning of the symbols. For example, the sixth chapter of Revelation describes the scroll with seven seals. Obviously the scroll and the seals are symbolic descriptions of future events. However, the descriptions of what will happen as each of the seals is broken are literal prophecies.

The first seal describes the emergence of the world ruler. Although some interpreters believe the world ruler will take power at the beginning of the seven years—that is, immediately following the Rapture—end-time prophecy as a whole indicates this will take place at the beginning of the three and a half year period immediately preceding the second coming of Christ. The passage concerning the first seal describes the world ruler as a conqueror: "And I looked, and behold, a white horse. And he who sat on it had a bow; and a crown was given to him, and he went out conquering and to conquer" (v. 2). A white horse is symbolic of a victorious general. Significantly this conqueror rides forth with a bow, but no arrow. The absence of an arrow indicates he will gain control of the world government by proclamation rather than by war.

The description of the second seal reveals, however, that there will be war and peace will be taken from the world (vv. 3–4). The symbolic breaking of the third seal reveals the next literal event: famine (vv. 5–6).

The fourth seal describes a devastating judgment that will kill a fourth of the earth's population:

> When He opened the fourth seal, I heard the voice of the fourth living creature saying, "Come and see." So I looked, and behold, a pale horse. And the name of him who sat on it was Death, and Hades followed with him. And power was given to them over a fourth of the earth, to kill with sword, with hunger, with death, and by the beasts of the earth.   (vv. 7–8)

Although the pale horse and the figure named Death are symbolic, the remainder of this description is a literal prophecy that one-fourth of the earth's population will die by sword, famine, plague, and attacks from wild beasts. This is not symbolic, but a literal prophecy.

The fifth seal refers to those who will be martyred during the tribulation (vv. 9–11), and the sixth seal describes a great earthquake, affecting not only the planet, but the stars, sun, and moon as well. Although some scholars have tried to interpret this prophecy symbolically, it is best understood as a literal description of catastrophes that will occur in the natural world and will result in great loss of life and physical destruction of the earth (vv. 12–14). These events will be the result of God's wrath (v. 17), making clear that the various judgments previously described will result also from the wrath of God. These judgments will be directed toward Israel and those who choose not to believe and accept the way of salvation, but all who are living during that time will suffer. However, God has promised that His church will not experience His wrath (1 Thess. 5:4). Therefore, the church will be raptured before "the great day of His wrath" begins (Rev. 6:17).

The idea that God would leave the church on earth and somehow protect believers from the awful consequences of His wrath is not borne out by the book of Revelation. The nature of the judgments, such as devastation by sword, famine, plague, and attack by wild beasts, does not separate the unsaved from the saved, but applies equally to all people regardless of their belief. Furthermore, Revelation 12 states that at the beginning of the latter three and a half years Satan will be cast out of heaven, where he is presently accusing the brethren. His role will be to persecute Jews, the woman referred to in 12:1, and Christians (vv. 7–12). Therefore, those living at that time who will become believers after the Rapture will have the double jeopardy of being persecuted by the world ruler, who will attempt to put every Christian and Jew to death, as well as the natural catastrophes which will befall the world as a whole. Consequently, in the Great Tribulation Christians who are saved after the Rapture will have less chance of surviving than non-Christians.

Revelation 7:9–17 describes a great multitude in heaven who will be martyred during the Great Tribulation and before the Second Coming. These are the individuals who will refuse to worship the beast and will have the special resurrection referred to in Revelation 20:4–6. This passage supports the idea that they are in heaven before the Second Coming, because they were martyred. After the Second Coming they will be resurrected and will be in the millennial earth.

In answering the disciples' questions concerning signs of the end, Christ said the Great Tribulation would begin with the desecration of the temple—the event Daniel called the "abomination of desolation" (Dan. 11:31; 12:11)—and would be the first sign of the Second Coming (Matt. 24:15–28). Christ described this time as one of great tribulation, saying: "For then there will be great tribulation, such as has not been since the beginning of the world until this time, no, nor ever shall be" (v. 21). He also said this period will be so awful that no one would survive if He did not come again and rescue the remnants: "And unless those days were shortened, no flesh would be saved; but for the elect's sake those days will be shortened" (v. 22).

The seventh seal reveals the sounding of seven trumpets (Rev. 8:1–9:21; 11:15–19). These trumpets signal devastating worldwide judgments that extend to a third of the earth and cause great loss of life and property. The sixth trumpet introduces an invasion of the Holy Land by an Eastern military force of 200 million (Rev. 9:11). This force apparently will participate in the final war in Israel, and the invaders will have the power to kill a third of mankind (v. 9:15).

As the fourth seal prophesies the death of one-fourth the peoples of the world, half the world's population will have perished after the sixth trumpet. It is clear that at this point the Great Tribulation will be well under way.

The sounding of the seventh trumpet introduces a final series of seven events called "bowls of wrath." These events are similar to those signaled by the trumpets, but the destruction that results from each is worldwide, rather than limited to one-third of the earth. The result of the first judgment will be painful sores on the people who worship the world ruler (Rev. 16:2). The second bowl prophesies that the waters of the seas will turn into blood and cause every living thing in the sea to die. The third bowl reveals that the rivers will turn to blood. The fourth bowl indicates a change in the earth's climate to a great heat never known before: "Then the fourth angel poured out his bowl on the sun, and power was given to him to scorch men with fire. And men were scorched with great heat, and they blasphemed the name of God who has power over these plagues; and they did not repent and give him glory" (16:8). The pouring out of the fifth bowl will bring darkness to the world and pain to the human race.

The sixth bowl describes what will happen to the great river Euphrates. It will dry up and the kings of the East—the great army mentioned in the sixth trumpet— will be able to invade the land of Israel. Following the sixth bowl, the war in Armageddon will occur. This will be the final great world war.

> And I saw three unclean spirits like frogs coming out of the mouth of the dragon, out of the mouth of the beast, and out of the mouth of the false prophet. For they are spirits of demons, performing signs, which go out to the kings of the earth and of the whole world, to gather them to the battle of that great day of God Almighty. "Behold, I am coming as a thief. Blessed is he who watches, and keeps his garments, lest he walk naked and they see his shame." And then they gathered them together to the place called in Hebrew, Armageddon (vv. 13–16).

Scripture calls this war "the battle of that great day of God Almighty" (v. 14). In popular terminology it is known as the battle of Armageddon because it will center at the Mount of Megiddo located in northern Israel, known in Aramaic as Armageddon. Actually, as other Scriptures describe this scene (for example, Daniel 11:40–45), both the invading and the defending armies will probably be dispersed all over the land of Israel, which will be some 200 miles from north to south and will extend from the Mediterranean on the west all the way to the Euphrates River to the east. The army from the Orient alone will number 200 million men (9:16). These armies will engage in a war for world power against the world ruler as the world crumbles under the various judgments of God. The war, however, will be unresolved, and even on the day of the Second Coming there will be house-to-house fighting in Jerusalem (Zech. 14:1–3).

Revelation describes one final bowl that will be poured out before the Second Coming occurs. Verses 17 through 21 of the sixteenth chapter describe a devastating world-wide earthquake. It will destroy Babylon (see Rev. 18), "the cities of the nations" will collapse (v. 16–19), and islands and mountains will disappear (v. 20). The judgment of the earthquake will climax in a supernatural hailstorm in which the stones will weigh a hundred pounds each (v. 21). The world will be in shambles and its cities will be in ruins. Apparently only Jerusalem and the cities of Israel will be left unscathed.

It is to this scene that Christ will return in power and glory, as described in Revelation 19:11–16.

The Great Tribulation Is a Literal Prophecy

While there is some symbolism in the descriptions of the Great Tribulation, the events are frequently described in very plain language. Therefore, one thing is quite clear: These events will be an awful judgment on a Christ-rejecting world. A world that worships Satan and the ruler he substitutes for Christ will merit the judgments God will pour out. The Great Tribulation will be the most awful destruction of human life and property ever to occur in history, and it will prelude the second coming of Christ.

The devastation prophesied for the tribulation makes it very difficult for posttribulationists to substantiate the idea that the church could possibly move through this period unscathed. Certainly a rapture at the end of this period would be a "blessed hope" that the suffering would end, but the blessed hope of the Rapture is that the church will be removed *before* the awful judgments begin. Furthermore, there is no mention of a rapture in connection with events leading directly to the Second Coming or the Second Coming itself. The resurrection of the martyred dead (Rev. 20:4–6) and the resurrection of Old Testament saints (Dan. 12:1–2) will occur some time after the Second Coming, not while Christ is in the air.

Scripture does not substantiate the arguments of those who want to ignore or explain away the literal character of the tribulation. It will occur after the Rapture and before the Second Coming, and it will be awful.

—— 11 ——

THE ELEVENTH KEY

The Second Coming

The Second Coming will fulfill many Old and New Testament Scriptures. The first of these prophecies is recorded in Deuteronomy in Moses' final instructions to the children of Israel:

> Now it shall come to pass, when all these things come upon you, the blessing and the curse which I have set before you, and you call them to mind among all the nations where the LORD your God drives you, and you return to the LORD your God and obey His voice, according to all that I command you today, you and your children, with all your heart and with all your soul, that the LORD your God will bring you back from captivity, and have compassion on you, and gather you again from all the nations where the LORD your God has scattered you. If any of you are driven out to the farthest parts under heaven, from there the LORD your God will gather you, and from there He will bring you. Then the LORD your God will bring you to the land which your fathers possessed, and you shall possess it. He will prosper you and multiply you more than your fathers. (Deut. 30:1–5)

(The King James version adds "and will return" to verse 3: "Then the LORD thy God will turn thy captivity, and have compassion upon thee, and will return and gather thee . . .") Moses also described how the Lord will delight in them, bless them spiritually, and make them prosperous with good crops (vv. 6–9).

It is most significant that in this first prophecy of the Second Coming, Christ's return is related to Israel's restoration, regathering, and installation in the Promised Land. This is a prominent theme of the Old Testament and a major factor in prophecies concerning the Second Coming (see, for example, Jer. 23:5–8 and the Scripture passages referred to in chapter 2). Many of the Psalms, such as Psalm 22, 24, 50, 72, 96, and 110, prophesy Christ's second coming and the kingdom that will follow. Daniel 7:13–14 says Christ's coming will signal the beginning of His reign on earth:

> I was watching in the night visions,
> And behold, One like the Son of Man,
> Coming with the clouds of heaven!
> He came to the Ancient of Days,
> And they brought Him near before Him.
> Then to Him was given dominion and glory and a kingdom,
> That all peoples, nations, and languages should serve Him.
> His dominion is an everlasting dominion,
> Which shall not pass away,
> And His kingdom the one
> Which shall not be destroyed.

Other prophets, such as Isaiah, also picture the future government of Christ as one of peace that will have no end:

> Of the increase of His government and peace
> There will be no end,
> Upon the throne of David and over His kingdom,
> To order it and establish it with judgment and justice
> From that time forward, even forever.
> The zeal of the LORD of hosts will perform this. (Isa. 9:7)

Throughout the Old Testament the Second Coming is associated with Christ's future reign on David's throne, as well as His universal government over all nations. Many passages, such as those found in the Minor Prophets, describe the kingdom on earth which will follow the Second Coming. For example, Zechariah describes Christ interrupting the war in Israel, even as invaders are destroying Jerusalem:

> Then the LORD will go forth
> And fight against those nations,
> As He fights in the day of battle.

And in that day His feet will stand on the Mount of Olives,
Which faces Jerusalem on the east.
And the Mount of Olives shall be split in two,
From east to west,
Making a very large valley;
Half of the mountain shall move toward the north
And half of it toward the south.   (Zech. 14:3–4)

A following passage describes the changes that will take place in Jerusalem:

And the LORD shall be King over all the earth.
In that day it shall be—
"The LORD is one,"
And His name one.   (v. 9)

The New Testament reveals more about the Second Coming. In response to the disciples' questions about the time of His return, Christ dramatically described the event and said He would come again following the Great Tribulation:

For as the lightning comes from the east and flashes to the west, so also will the coming of the Son of Man be. For wherever the carcass is, there the eagles will be gathered together. Immediately after the tribulation of those days the sun will be darkened, and the moon will not give its light; the stars will fall from heaven, and the powers of the heavens will be shaken. Then the sign of the Son of Man will appear in heaven, and then all the tribes of the earth will mourn, and they will see the Son of Man coming on the clouds of heaven with power and great glory. (Matt. 24:27–30)

Many other passages refer to Christ's second coming or to events that will follow it which require His return to earth as a prelude. Some scholars have estimated that one out of every twenty-five verses in the New Testament refers either to the Second Coming or to the rapture of the church. (See chapter 2.)

Scripture describes Christ as wearing "a robe dipped in blood," and tells us "His name is called The Word of God" (Rev. 19:13). The hosts of heaven will ride on white horses, (symbolic of victory) and be dressed in "fine linen, white and clean" (symbolic of righteousness) (v. 19:14).

The Second Coming, unlike the Rapture, will be a time of judgment and Christ will come for this purpose: "Now out of His mouth goes a sharp sword, that with it He should strike the nations. And He Himself will rule them with a rod of iron. He Himself treads the winepress of the fierceness and wrath of Almighty God" (v. 15). The fact that the Second Coming concerns the Lord Jesus is made clear in the statement, "And He has on His robe and on His thigh a name written: KING OF KINGS AND LORD OF LORDS" (v. 16).

Notice how completely different this description of the Second Coming is from the details of the rapture of the church given in 1 Thessalonians 4:13–18. The myriad details and the purpose of the Second Coming are in direct contrast to the simple procedure of taking the church from the world to heaven.

The purpose of Christ's return to earth is revealed in the revelation that follows. Believing that power will go to the victors, Satan will have assembled great armies to fight each other. He will also have marshalled these armies for the express purpose of concentrating all the military might of the world in the Holy Land in anticipation of Christ's return (vv. 13–14). When the Second Coming begins the armies will join together to fight against the armies of heaven.

Christ will speak and, according to Revelation 19:15, out of His mouth will come a sharp sword. Satan's armies will be killed instantly and their beasts also. The carnage described in Revelation 19:17–18 paints an awful picture of destruction:

> Then I saw an angel standing in the sun; and he cried with a loud voice, saying to all the birds that fly in the midst of heaven, "Come and gather together for the supper of the great God, that you may eat the flesh of kings, the flesh of captains, the flesh of mighty men, the flesh of horses and of those who sit on them, and the flesh of all people, free and slave, both small and great."

The description of this "supper of the great God," when the bodies of the wicked will be destroyed, is in direct contrast to the wedding supper described in verse 9, which is a worshipful celebration.

Following the destruction of the armies, the world rulers, described as "the beast" and the "false prophet" (vv. 19–20), will be captured and "cast alive into the lake of fire burning with brimstone" (v. 20; see also Matt. 25:41). Verse 21 summarizes the fulfillment of this dreadful judgment: "And the rest were killed with the sword which proceeded from the mouth of Him who sat on the horse. And all the birds were filled with their flesh."

The events described in chapter 20, verses 1–3, are the natural cause and effect result of the Second Coming. However, interpreters are divided in their opinions of the meaning. Some scholars, especially those who are amillenarian, try to relate this portion of the text to Christ's first coming. But there is no textual justification for that interpretation. With the armies disposed of and the beast and false prophet "cast alive into the lake of fire burning with brimstone," the natural result of the Second Coming is the binding of Satan.

John records that the binding of Satan was revealed to him:

> Then I saw an angel coming down from heaven, having the key to the bottomless pit and a great chain in his hand. He laid hold of the dragon, that serpent of old, who is the Devil and Satan, and bound him for a thousand years; and he cast him into the bottomless pit, and shut him up, and set a seal on him, so that he should deceive the nations no more till the thousand years were finished. But after these things he must be released for a little while. (Rev. 20:1–3)

An important perspective of this passage is gained by recognizing that it describes what John *saw* as well as what he *heard*. What he saw could be subject to interpretation. John saw an angel with a key to the bottomless pit—the home of the demon world. John saw the angel seize the dragon, who is clearly identified as the devil or Satan, throw him into the bottomless pit, and lock and seal it.

The purpose of this action, however, could not be revealed to John visually. Therefore, he was told the purpose and what he heard must be accepted literally. John heard that Satan would be bound for a thousand years (v. 2), so that he "should deceive the nations no longer" until after the thousand years are finished (v. 3).

This literal interpretation is firmly resisted by the amillenarians who do not want to accept a thousand-year millennial kingdom following the Second Coming. They want instead to foster the idea that this passage, as well as others, means that Satan was bound at the first coming of Christ and is unable in the present age to "deceive the nations."

Although obviously Satan was defeated at the cross, the idea that he is inoperative today is simply not supported by the facts of history or by Scripture. The New Testament describes Satan as very much alive and active, calling him "an angel of light" (2 Cor. 11:14) and warning us that he "walks about like a roaring lion, seeking whom he may devour" (1 Peter 5:8).

The natural and obvious interpretation of Revelation 20:1-3 is that Satan is operative today but will be bound at the Second Coming. He will remain imprisoned and unable to continue his terrible work of opposing God for the one thousand years of the millennial kingdom.

Revelation 20:4-6 describes the resurrection of those who will be martyred during the Great Tribulation only a year or two before the Second Coming. The passage clearly states that the martyrs will be raised in order to reign with Christ for a thousand years (v. 4). Obviously that period must follow the martyrs' resurrection. The passage also clearly states that the wicked dead will not be resurrected until the thousand-year reign is finished (v. 5).

It is amazing that some orthodox scholars can defend a literal virgin birth, a literal deity of Christ, and a literal death and resurrection of Christ, but depart completely from literal interpretation when discussing the doctrine of the millennial kingdom. The facts revealed in the first six verses of Revelation 20 are not shrouded in symbolism or

otherwise difficult to interpret. The text is quite clear:
Following the Second Coming, there will be a thousand-
year period during which time the righteous dead of the
tribulation will be resurrected to be present with the
righteous of past generations, who have been either translated or resurrected. They will share in the millennial
kingdom of Christ. Furthermore, Satan will be bound
during this time and the wicked dead will not be resurrected until the thousand years has ended.

According to Daniel 7:13–14, the Second Coming will
signal the beginning of Christ's reign on earth and His
millennial kingdom which at its close will merge into the
eternal kingdom which, of course, will never end. At the
Second Coming He will return to Jerusalem (Zech. 14:1–
4), where His throne will be (Isa. 2:3–4), and when His feet
touch the Mount of Olives a valley will form, extending
from Jerusalem east to the Jordan River (Zech. 14:4). He
will be accompanied by ten thousands of saints to "execute
judgment" on all the world (Jude 1:14–15).

The most graphic picture of the Second Coming is recorded in Revelation 19:11–21 where Christ is described
as leading a great procession of angels and saints (the
armies in heaven) to claim the earth. As a result, the
armies of the world will be destroyed, the world ruler and
the false prophet will be cast into the lake of fire, and the
millennial reign of Christ will begin (Rev. 19:17–20:6).

The Second Coming stands in sharp contrast to the
rapture of the church. At the Second Coming there will
be no translation, no resurrection while he is in the air,
and no movement of the saints from earth to heaven. The
Second Coming is an event that terminates on earth and
will take many hours to unfold. During this time the earth
will revolve, making it possible for His coming to be witnessed by the entire world. In many respects the Second
Coming is the climax of history and the ultimate triumph
of Jesus Christ as King of kings and Lord of lords.

— 12 —

THE TWELFTH KEY
The Millennium

The English word *millennium* comes from the Latin word *mille*, meaning "thousand." The Greek word for millennium comes from *chilias*, meaning "a thousand," and *annus*, meaning "year." The Greek term is used six times in the original text of the twentieth chapter of Revelation to define the duration of Christ's kingdom on earth prior to the destruction of the old heavens and the old earth. Therefore, the word millennium refers to the thousand years of Christ's future reign on earth that will precede eternity.

The Doctrine

The doctrine of the millennium and how it should be interpreted has divided the church into three major factions—those who support the amillennial view, those who support the postmillennial view, and those who support the premillennial view—and the theologies of these groups are radically different. Because the doctrine is vitally important, the dissimilar interpretations each group employs to understand prophecy concerning the millennium determine their interpretation of many biblical prophecies.

Amillennialism

The amillennial view is basically non-millennial. It denies there will ever literally be a millennium.

At the close of the second century, the school of theology

at Alexandria, Egypt, first advanced the non-millennial interpretation of the millennial doctrine. The Alexandrian theologians argued that the millennial prophecies could not be considered literally and would have to be fulfilled in non-literal ways. Even though most theologians have since recognized the Alexandrian school was heretical, the Alexandrian non-millennial interpretation has dominated the church throughout history.

In the fourth and fifth centuries, Augustine redefined this interpretation with the idea that the millennial prophecies were being fulfilled in a spiritual kingdom as God rules in the hearts of believers in the present age. Although Augustine did not carry this interpretation so far as to set dates, some of his followers took his idea to mean the millennium would end in 1000 A.D. When this date passed, they decided the millennium was non-literal in length as well as in rule.

The Protestant reformers later corrected many of the misconceptions of the Roman Catholic Church, but they founded their understanding of prophecy on Augustine's teachings and more or less embraced his point of view. Accordingly over time the amillennialist interpretation of the doctrine of the millennium has been that it is being fulfilled in a non-literal way in the present world. This theology requires extensive non-literal interpretation of the many Old Testament passages that describe the millennial kingdom as well as the specific prophecies in Revelation 20.

Modern variations of amillennialism, which have not attracted many followers, include the idea that the millennium occurs in the intermediate state—the period between physical death and resurrection. A more recent idea is that the millennial kingdom will exist in the new heaven and new earth discussed in Revelation 21-22.

All amillennial theologies require a non-literal interpretation of many, but not all, prophetic Scripture. Amillenialists may continue to believe in a literal Second Coming, a literal resurrection, and a literal heaven and hell.

Postmillennialism

A particular variation of amillennialism became popular in the nineteenth century. This new interpretation suggested that the millennium would occur during the last one thousand years of the present age. Adherents argued that prophetic Scripture indicated the Gospel would be triumphant, winning the whole world to Christ. The millennium would then be an ideal or golden age lasting for one thousand years. This doctrinal interpretation is known as postmillennialism because it suggests that the Second Coming will occur after the millennium.

Obviously the current situation, in either the nineteenth century or the twentieth, is not a golden age. Therefore the adherents of this interpretation usually taught that the millennium was just about to begin. However, succeeding generations continually needed to advance the beginning date because the present age had not become "golden," nor did it appear to be actually moving in that direction.

The postmillennial interpretation is far more optimistic than the amillennial view since it teaches that Christ will at least reign spiritually on earth and mankind will embrace Christianity. However, the postmillennial view took a mortal blow in the twentieth century. Germany, the country where the Reformation was born, attacked other countries of Europe, bringing on World War I. At the same time it was obvious that the Gospel was not penetrating the entire world. Then World War II added further evidence that mankind in general was not growing more Christlike.

The postmillennial view has now been largely abandoned, although currently some Christians are attempting to revive it. Since relatively few people believe that the world is getting better and that Christianity will triumph over the secularism, the unbelief, and the ignorance of God inherent in our present world, this theology has little popularity today.

Premillennialism

The premillennial interpretation of the millennial doctrine states that the millennial kingdom will follow the Second Coming and will be literally fulfilled by a thousand-year reign of Christ on earth. This theology is founded on the principle that all prophecies mean what they state in a normal sense. Because many long passages in the Old Testament discuss the future kingdom and Revelation 20, as well as other New Testament passages, also discusses it at length, the premillennial interpretation is that the millennium will occur after Christ's second advent. This theology is based on the literal fulfillment of the prophecies of the book of Revelation as events described in chronological order in Chapters 19–22.

The debate between adherents of the different millennial interpretations continues today, although the amillennial view probably still predominates. Premillenarians continue to insist that the Bible teaches their interpretation and back their argument with a great deal of exegesis and data to confirm their theology. The discussion to follow supports the premillennial view and will attempt to prove that the Bible does not teach either the postmillennial or the amillennial interpretation.

The Millennium and the Second Coming

The book of Revelation reveals that the second coming of Christ will be a very dramatic event. The text describes a multitude of saints and angels proceeding from heaven to earth to establish Christ's earthly kingdom. Such an event would obviously be a dramatic intervention by God in human history. The results of this divine intervention are described in Revelation, principally in chapters 19 and 20.

According to Revelation 19:17–21, the armies of the world will be engaged in mighty battle for world power. When Christ appears, the earthly armies will immediately band together to fight His heavenly army. But Christ will speak—a "sharp sword" will come "out of His mouth" (19:15)—and the earthbound armies will be destroyed.

Then the beast (the world ruler described earlier in Revelation), and the false prophet (the world ruler's assistant), will be captured and cast into the lake of fire (19:20).

The text describes the events that will follow and appears to give them in chronological order. The premillennial interpretation is that the text describes events which logically result from the Second Coming, the events will follow one after the other in the order in which they are described, and the text does not indicate a passage of time between the events. Satan will be bound and cast into the abyss—the home of the demon world (20:1–3)— where he will remain for a thousand years, unable to "deceive the nations" during the millennium. At the end of the millennium, he will be released and eventually will receive his eternal judgment when he will be cast into the lake of fire (v. 10).

A logical, literal interpretation of these prophecies indicates a period of one thousand years will follow the Second Coming. And the text describes an event that will occur at the conclusion of the thousand years—Satan will be released and unbound, but then will be cast into the lake of fire to remain there forever.

Amillenarians attempt to explain away the implications of these prophecies by teaching that Satan was bound at the first coming of Christ and that the thousand-year period mentioned in the text is not a literal prophecy. However, these interpretations are not supported by either the text of Revelation or passages found elsewhere in the Bible.

The New Testament very clearly does not teach that Satan was bound at the first coming of Christ, even though he was defeated at the cross and his ultimate judgment was and remains assured. He is actually very alive and active in the world. At the present time he is not only able to accuse the saints in heaven, but to afflict people on earth. For example, evidence of his activities in the present age is in the descriptions of demon possession after the death of Christ and in 1 Peter 5:8, where Satan is described as one who "walks about like a roaring lion, seeking whom he may devour." Furthermore, 1 Peter 5:9 encourages Christians to "resist him, steadfast in the faith, knowing that the same sufferings are experienced by your brotherhood in the world." In other words, we are not to rest on the assumption that Satan is bound, but are to resist him and realize he is causing suffering among Christians around the world.

Scriptural evidence confirms that the binding of Satan is a realistic event of the future and will be a natural result of the second coming of Christ. Scriptural evidence also reveals the binding of Satan will be followed by the resurrection of the tribulation dead.

According to Revelation 20:4–6, the Christians who will be beheaded because they refuse to worship the beast will be resurrected in order to reign with Christ during the millennium:

> And I saw the souls of those who had been beheaded for their witness to Jesus and for the word of God, who had not worshiped the beast or his image, and had not received his mark on their foreheads or on their hands. And they lived and reigned with Christ for a thousand years. (20:4)

These martyrs are the Christians who will live a few years before Christ's second coming. They will refuse to worship the world ruler who claims to be God but is allied with Satan. According to Scripture, the believers who refuse to worship the world ruler will be beheaded and will form part of the great multitude of martyrs described in Revelation 7:9–17 who are in heaven as a result of the Great Tribulation. They will be resurrected following the binding of Satan.

The prophecy of the resurrection of the tribulation dead is further evidence that the Second Coming will be followed by an actual millennial kingdom on earth. The text describes the martyrs' being resurrected following the cessation of their suffering at the hand of the world ruler and after he has been cast into the lake of fire. Furthermore, the text specifically states the martyrs will be raised to reign a thousand years with Christ.

Those who embrace the amillennial and the postmillennial philosophies have difficulty incorporating these passages in their interpretation of the doctrine of the millennium. Generally they offer the explanation that the resurrection of the martyrs refers to the new birth of the believer in the present age. But the passage mentions nothing about new birth. Instead it describes the resurrection of believers who experienced physical death, and the text clearly places this event in the period that chronologically follows the Second Coming.

Revelation 20:5–6 gives additional evidence of the chronological events of the millennium and further substantiates arguments that it will literally occur. These verses state:

> But the rest of the dead did not live again until the thousand years were finished. This is the first resurrection. Blessed and holy is he who has part in the first resurrection. Over such the second death has no power, but they shall be priests of God and of Christ, and shall reign with Him a thousand years.

Obviously the "first resurrection" these verses refer to is not the first resurrection of history. There have been a number of resurrections already, including Christ's resurrection and the resurrection of the saints that occurred following Christ's crucifixion (Matt. 27:52–53). By the time of the Second Coming, other resurrections will have occurred also. The "dead in Christ" will have been resurrected at the Rapture and also the two witnesses whose resurrections are revealed in Revelation 11. All these resurrections will occur before this "first" resurrection of the millennial period.

This one is called "first" because in the context of the millennium it is first—at the beginning of the millennium. In contrast, the second resurrection—the time the "rest of the dead" will live again—will occur when the thousand years are finished. The "first resurrection" will be before the resurrection of the wicked and, therefore, is the first of this period.

Perhaps the most pointed evidence of the length of Christ's earthly kingdom is the revelation concerning the resurrected martyrs of the tribulation. They will be delivered from the power of death and will reign with Christ for a thousand years. They will have been killed only a year or two before the Second Coming. In the context of the passage, the reign begins after their resurrection, and verse 11 of chapter 19 reveals that the Second Coming will have already occurred when this resurrection takes place some days after the Second Coming.

Verse 7 of chapter 20 states, "Now when the thousand years have expired, Satan will be released from his prison." Verses 8–10 reveal Satan will stir up a rebellion against God among those in the millennial kingdom who were born in the millennium and never really trusted Christ. Then Satan will receive his ultimate judgment and will be cast "into the lake of fire and brimstone where the beast and the false prophet are. And they will be tormented day and night forever and ever."

Revelation 19 and 20 describe the events that will precede the millennium: Christ will return, the armies will be destroyed, the beast and the false prophet will be cast into the lake of fire, Satan will be bound, and the tribulation martyrs will be resurrected. These two chapters also describe the events that will occur at the millennium's end, one thousand years later: Satan will be loosed, he will "go out to deceive the nations," he will receive his final judgment in the lake of fire, and the wicked dead will be resurrected and judged and will experience the second death. Chapter 21 reveals that when all these events have occurred, the first heaven and the first earth will pass away and the new heaven and new earth will be created.

Revelation 20:4–6 confirms that the Rapture will not occur at the Second Coming, for the resurrection of the tribulation martyrs will occur some days after Christ returns in contrast to the church which will be raptured years before He returns. If the Rapture were to occur at the time of the Second Coming or immediately before, the tribulation dead would also be resurrected at that time.

The amillennialist and postmillennialist theologies leave no room for a millennium. However, understood with the natural meaning of the language, these prophecies clearly teach a millennial kingdom on earth following the second coming of Christ and lasting for one thousand years.

The Millennium and the Promised Land

The promise of the Land (Gen. 12:7) is one of the important arguments in favor of a literal interpretation of millennial prophecy. History reveals that this promise which God made to Abraham has not been completely fulfilled; therefore, some of the prophecy must be fulfilled in the future. Just as God rescued the children of Israel from Egypt, Babylon, and Assyria, as He promised to, He will regather them, as He said He will, from all over the world and allow them to occupy the Promised Land with the partitions indicated in Ezekiel 47–48. Many Scripture passages testify to this fact and indicate this great event will climax at the second coming of Christ.

All the Scripture passages concerning God's covenant with Abraham about the Land have no meaning, however, when considered from the amillennial and postmillennial perspectives. These theologies leave no room for the future territorial revival of Israel; neither do they allow the fulfillment of the prophecy of God's new covenant with Israel (Jer. 31:31–37). But, because God's Word needs to be fulfilled, the restoration of Israel is necessary for the fulfillment of the promise of a new covenant.

The Bible has many, many references explaining that Israel, although she is presently scattered all over the world in unbelief, will experience spiritual and territorial restoration. Absolutely essential to the nation's restoration is the future millennial kingdom, for if the millennial kingdom does not occur, the prophecies cannot be fulfilled.

Connected to the fulfillment of the promise of the Land for Israel is the promise that the curse on mankind

brought about by Adam's sin will be lifted, at least partially. Isaiah is quite clear about that:

> The wilderness and the wasteland shall be glad for them,
> And the desert shall rejoice and blossom as the rose;
> It shall blossom abundantly and rejoice,
> Even with joy and singing.
> The glory of Lebanon shall be given to it,
> The excellence of Carmel and Sharon.
> They shall see the glory of the LORD,
> The excellency of our God.   (Isa. 35:1–2)

In contrast to the drought many areas have today,
ample rainfall will come upon the earth in the millennial
kingdom (Isa. 30:23; 35:7). This will allow cattle to thrive
and an abundance of food to grow (Isa. 30:23–24). Since
the curse on the earth will be only partially lifted, there
will still be physical death, although apparently life spans
will be longer. In fact, Isaiah 65 describes an individual
who is dying at the age of 100 as young (v. 20).

The land will experience tremendous changes. At the
time of the Second Coming, the Mount of Olives will divide,
as stated in Zechariah 14:4:

> And in that day His feet will stand on the Mount of Olives,
> Which faces Jerusalem on the east.
> And the Mount of Olives shall be split in two,
> From east to west,
> Making a very large valley;
> Half of the mountain shall move toward the north
> And half of it toward the south.

Other catastrophic changes will occur, as described in
Zechariah 14:8, and the water will move in unusual pat-
terns:

> And in that day it shall be
> That living waters shall flow from Jerusalem,
> Half of them toward the eastern sea
> And half of them toward the western sea;
> In both summer and winter it shall occur.

Apparently the abundance of water will also overrun the
Dead Sea and carry fresh water all the way to the South.
In addition land elevations around Jerusalem will alter:

"The whole land, from Geba to Rimmon, south of Jerusalem, will become like the Arabah. But Jerusalem will be raised up and remain in its place, from the Benjamin Gate to the site of the First Gate, to the Corner Gate and from the Tower of Hananel to the royal winepresses. It will be inhabited; never again will it be destroyed. Jerusalem will be secure" (vv. 10–11 NIV). The abundance of water will restore plants and trees and apparently fish will thrive.

Obviously in all of history none of these particular predictions have been fulfilled. If they are to be fulfilled, a millennial kingdom will be essential. Amillenarians are forced either to ignore these prophecies or to try to explain them away with some sort of non-literal fulfillment in the present age.

These prophecies about the millennial kingdom form a foundation for the doctrine of Israel's restoration (see chapter 6). The details of the millennial kingdom and its special features confirm the proper approach to prophetic interpretation and the concept that the millennial prophecies will be fulfilled literally.

The Millennium and David's Kingdom

God's covenant with David is one of the major biblical covenants, and the future Davidic kingdom is of prime importance to the complete fulfillment of the Davidic Covenant. Therefore, consideration of the Davidic Covenant and the future Davidic kingdom are essential to studying both the future of Israel and prophecy concerning the millennium.

As discussed in chapter 3, the kingdom of David will be restored in the millennium, Christ will assume the throne of David (Ps. 89:1–4, 20–37), and He will rule over the house of Israel as well as over the whole world (Ps. 72). Christ will reign from Jerusalem (Isa. 2:3), and in the new earth following the millennium His reign will last for all eternity (Ps. 89). Jeremiah 23:5–8 says Christ will reign over Judah and Israel at His second coming, and the nation Israel will be brought back to their Promised Land.

These Scriptures combined with many other passages affirm that the promise to reestablish David's kingdom and its government will have its ultimate fulfillment in the millennial kingdom prior to the eternal state. The kingdom rule of Christ will, of course, greatly affect the millennial period and will inaugurate a righteous government that will bring much blessing to the people of the world. An important aspect of Christ's presence in the millennial kingdom is that He will be physically and visibly present. That should do much to advance the cause of God in the world and make unreasonable any unbelief in Christ as God and as Savior.

Major Features of the Millennium

Many facets of the millennial kingdom will improve upon the present age. A number of the unique features will relate to spiritual life as Christ's physical presence will be the visual revelation of God's glory. Scripture is clear that all the adults who enter the millennial kingdom will be saved, and the unsaved will be purged, whether they are Israelite or Gentile. Children will, of course, enter the millennium without judgment, and during the millennium many others will be born.

Because of Christ's presence, the earth will abound in the knowledge of the LORD: "For the earth shall be full of the knowledge of the LORD as the waters cover the sea" (Isa. 11:9). At the beginning of the millennium every adult will not only be saved but indwelt by the Spirit of God. There is also evidence that many will be filled with the Spirit, perhaps more so than at any one time ever before (Isa. 32:15; 44:3; Ezek. 36:26; 37:14; 39:29; Joel 2:28–29).

A part of the blessing of the new Covenant is the promise that God will speak to the hearts of the saved:

> "But this is the covenant that I will make with the house of Israel after those days, says the LORD: I will put My law in their minds, and write it on their hearts; and I will be their God, and they shall be My people. No more shall every man teach his neighbor, and every man his brother, saying, 'Know the LORD,' for they all shall know Me, from

the least of them to the greatest of them," says the LORD. "For I will forgive their iniquity, and their sin I will remember no more."   (Jer. 31:33–34)

And their spiritual lives will be changed:

> For I will take you from among the nations, gather you out of all countries, and bring you into your own land. Then I will sprinkle clean water on you, and you shall be clean; I will cleanse you from all your filthiness and from all your idols. I will give you a new heart and put a new spirit within you; I will take the heart of stone out of your flesh and give you a heart of flesh. I will put My Spirit within you and cause you to walk in My statutes, and you will keep My judgments and do them.   (Ezek. 36:24–27)

Obviously, in the millennial kingdom there will be no hindrance to preaching God's word and every school will be a Bible school.

The Temple

One of the unusual features of the millennial kingdom will be the millennial temple, described in detail in Ezekiel 40:1–46:24. Amillenarians have great difficulty trying to explain this passage. The temple description does not correspond to any temple built in the past, although amillenarians try to link this description to one of the temples of history. However, Scripture makes clear that the temple described in this passage is much larger and different in function and design from any ever built. And the architectural details are too specific for this passage to symbolically represent something else. Just as the millennial kingdom itself will literally occur, so also the temple will be literal.

Those who understand the temple prophecy as a description of a temple that will literally exist in the millennial kingdom, however, have a problem with it. The temple is designed to facilitate animal sacrifices. Consequently a question naturally arises: Why would animal sacrifices be necessary in a future millennial kingdom when Christ has died and satisfied all the requirements of Old Testament sacrifices? To understand, the reader of

Scripture must bow to what the Bible actually says. Not only does Ezekiel refer to the sacrifices, but passages elsewhere in the Bible teach the same principles, for example, Isaiah 56:7; 66:20–23; Jeremiah 33:18; Zechariah 14:16–21; and Malachi 3:3–4. All these prophecies together give certain proof that the sacrifices will literally occur. How can this be explained?

The first principle to keep clearly in mind is that sacrifices were God's idea, not man's. God designed animal sacrifices to cause the people to look forward to the cross and Christ's sacrifice there. The Mosaic Covenant, which required men to sacrifice animals, was abolished by Christ's sacrifice. The situation in the millennium, although similar, will be different. Apparently, the explanation is that in the millennial kingdom, because the circumstances of mankind will be more ideal and people will be less likely to sin, the people will need a forceful reminder that Christ died to ensure their salvation. In much the way the Lord's Supper is observed in the present age as a memorial to the death of Christ, so the sacrifices of the millennium will be memorial but no more efficacious than were the sacrifices of the Old Testament. Just as sacrifices in Old Testament times looked forward to the sacrifice of Christ, so the millennial sacrifices will look back to it. People will need a pointed reminder of the necessity of Christ's death and God's grace in making the salvation of Christians possible, even in the ideal circumstances of the millennial kingdom.

Righteousness and Justice

Because Christ will reign from Jerusalem as King of kings and Lord of lords, justice will be inherent in the administration of God's laws in the millennial kingdom. Isaiah 11 declares this justice will be universal:

And He shall not judge by the sight of His eyes,
Nor decide by the hearing of His ears;
But with righteousness He shall judge the poor,
And decide with equity for the meek of the earth;
He shall strike the earth with the rod of His mouth,

And with the breath of His lips He shall slay the wicked.
Righteousness shall be the belt of His loins,
And faithfulness the belt of His waist.   (vv. 3–5)

Worldwide peace will also be a condition of the millennial kingdom:

He shall judge between the nations,
And shall rebuke many people;
They shall beat their swords into plowshares,
And their spears into pruning hooks;
Nation shall not lift up sword against nation,
Neither shall they learn war anymore.   (Isa. 2:4)

Psalm 72 provides a picture of the millennium revealing that Christ's glorious reign over all nations will bring blessings to all peoples.

Health and Prosperity

The millennium will be an ideal age so far as health and prosperity are concerned. Psalm 72:7 states,

In His days the righteous shall flourish,
And abundance of peace,
Until the moon is no more.

Many other Scripture passages confirm the period of plenty and prosperity in the millennial kingdom (Jer. 31:12; Ezek. 34:25–27; Joel 2:21–27; Amos 9:13–14). Because the earth will bring forth abundantly and taxation for military expenditures will be unnecessary, there will be more freedom with material things than ever before. Isaiah 65:21–23 describes civilization as one of equity, where houses can be built and the people will not be dispossessed. People who labor will not do so in vain:

And My elect shall long enjoy the work of their hands.
They shall not labor in vain,
Nor bring forth children for trouble;
For they shall be the descendants of the blessed of the LORD,
And their offspring with them.   (Isa. 65:22–23)

Along with general prosperity, good health will flourish, and physical disabilities will be largely unknown. Apparently, those who are sick will experience healing: "In that day the deaf shall hear the words of the book, and the eyes

of the blind shall see out of obscurity and out of darkness"
(Isa. 29:18). According to Isaiah 33:24, "No one living in
Zion will say, 'I am ill'; and the sins of those who dwell
there will be forgiven" (NIV).

We find another picture of general prosperity and
health in Isaiah 35:5–6:

> Then the eyes of the blind shall be opened,
> And the ears of the deaf shall be unstopped.
> Then the lame shall leap like a deer,
> And the tongue of the dumb sing.
> For waters shall burst forth in the wilderness,
> And streams in the desert.

As a result of the Great Tribulation, the earth's population will have been decimated, but during the millennium
population will rapidly increase:

> Then out of them shall proceed thanksgiving
> And the voice of those who make merry;
> I will multiply them, and they shall not diminish;
> I will also glorify them . . .
> And their congregation shall be established before Me;
> And I will punish all who oppress them.   (Jer. 30:19–20)

Even the Gentiles will enjoy the blessings of God and
physical health (Ezek. 47:22).

The Literalism of these Prophecies

The events prophesied for the millennium demonstrate
that no matter how ideal the circumstances, men will still
sin, even though Satan is inactive. In spite of the overwhelming evidence of Christ's power to save, not every one
will accept Him as Lord and Savior. At the close of the
millennium, when Satan is unbound, men and women will
follow him in a final rebellion against God, and God will
judge them.

The prophecies concerning these events are quite clear.
Still, in spite of the abundance of factual information
presented in the prophetic Word, some people deny the
evidence. It seems incredible that anyone can brush this
evidence aside and argue that the millennial kingdom will
not happen. Obviously the events of the present age have

not fulfilled these prophecies; neither can they be fulfilled in the eternal state. These prophecies clearly reveal that even though there will be prosperity, in the final events of history there will be death, sin, and final judgment. These things would not be possible in the eternal state, for in it there will be no sin and no death. There will be only the overwhelming results of God's grace.

Throughout time, from the Garden of Eden until the end of the millennium, God continually demonstrates in every age that salvation is only by His grace. Apart from the death of Christ there is no salvation, no forgiveness, no hope for the future. With the revelation of God's grace, the millennial kingdom is His triumphant dealing with human sin and His blessing for His people.

The millennial kingdom is the only possible fulfillment of these prophecies.

13

THE THIRTEENTH KEY

The Resurrections and the Final Judgment

The primary reason many scholars err when interpreting prophecy is that they attempt to merge all the resurrections and all the judgments described in the Bible into one great event. Posttribulationists add to the confusion by interpreting Revelation 20:5, which mentions "the first resurrection," as evidence that the Rapture will take place at the Second Coming. These arguments characterize the amillennial interpretation of Scripture which avoids any special attention to Israel and any statements that could possibly imply a future millennium.

Careful study of Scripture that discusses resurrections and judgments, however, reveals a series of resurrections and also a series of judgments widely separated by time, each occurring in a particular situation. Taken literally Revelation 20:4–6 clearly refers to a resurrection (the first) at the beginning of the period following the Second Coming and another resurrection (the second death) at the end of the millennium, one thousand years later.

A proper explanation of the "first resurrection" in the Revelation 20 passage, therefore, is that the term refers to the first one in a particular period, not the first resurrection of all time. This interpretation is often found in pretribulationist materials, but posttribulationists ignore this and proceed on the basis that "first" means number one. The meaning of the Revelation reference to "the first resurrection" becomes clear as the Bible unfolds the subject of resurrection.

The First Resurrection

The first resurrection in history was Christ's which occurred some 1,900 years ago. A number of people were restored to life before Christ was resurrected, but they were restored to their earthly bodies which would die again at a later time. In contrast Christ was resurrected in an eternal body that will never die.

Christ died on the cross to satisfy God's divine judgment against mankind's sin, as prophesied throughout the Old Testament. Consequently believers are justified through faith as revealed by many passages in the New Testament, such as Paul's reference in 1 Corinthians 15:3–4: "For I delivered to you first of all that which I also received: that Christ died for our sins according to the Scriptures, and that He was buried, and that He rose again the third day according to the Scriptures."

This resurrection is recorded in all four Gospels and is referred to many times throughout the New Testament as a past event. Therefore, obviously the first resurrection was Christ's and not "the first" referred to by Revelation 20:5.

The Second Resurrection

A second resurrection occurred immediately following Christ's. It is mentioned briefly and without comment in Matthew 27:51–53: "and the earth quaked, and the rocks were split, and the graves were opened; and many bodies of the saints who had fallen asleep were raised; and coming out of the graves after His resurrection, they went into the holy city and appeared to many."

A careful reading of this passage reveals that the graves of many of the saints who had died were opened as an earthquake occurred when Christ died. Those raised from the dead came out of their graves after Jesus arose three days following His death on the cross, and then they appeared in the city.

This event is not mentioned specifically elsewhere in the New Testament, but it fulfills the typology of the feasts of the Lord described in Leviticus 23. Verses 9 through 14 direct the people to bring a handful of grain to the priest at the beginning of the harvest season as a token of the coming harvest. According to verse 12, they were to offer a sacrifice or a burnt offering and, according to verse 13, a grain offering and a drink offering. Then, fifty days later when the harvest was complete, they were to bring a second offering which would recognize the harvest.

The point is that they were instructed to bring a sheaf of grain as a token, not a single stalk. Accordingly it is fitting that when Christ rose from the dead there would also be a token resurrection of a few as evidence of all future resurrections.

Scripture does not reveal what happened to those who were raised from the dead. However, inasmuch as they are the illustration of the resurrection of Christ, and the many resurrections that will occur because of his victory over death, it may be assumed they received eternal bodies that will never die, and that they ascended to heaven when their testimonies were finished.

The Third Resurrection

The third resurrection will occur at the Rapture. First Thessalonians 4:13–18 and 1 Corinthians 15:51–58 state that at the Rapture Christians who have died will be resurrected and their souls, which will be brought from heaven by Christ when He comes (1 Thess. 4:14), will enter their immortal bodies (2 Cor. 15:51–52). A moment later living Christians will be translated (1 Thess. 4:17), and will receive new bodies that will not be sinful, mortal, or subject to aging or decay. Those raised from the dead, as well as those among the living who will be changed, will meet Christ in the air (1 Thess. 4:17). In fulfillment of the promise Christ gave to His disciples recorded in John 14:3, He will take the raptured and resurrected Christians to His Father's house which is heaven.

The Rapture will be an important event of movement from earth to heaven following the resurrection of all Christians who have died and the translation of those Christians who are living in the world at that time.

The First Judgment

There is a sense in which Christ Himself experienced the first judgment when He died on the cross. However, Christians will have a judgment after the Rapture. This judgment of the church is one of the great doctrines relating to Christian life. Paul said, "You know that your labor in the Lord is not in vain" (1 Cor. 15:58 NIV) and "we must all appear before the judgment seat of Christ, that each one may receive what is due him for the things done while in the body, whether good or bad" (2 Cor. 5:10 NIV). This judgment will concern rewards, not sin. It will relate to what the Christian accomplished in life, and the words *good* and *bad* refer to value, not morality. Only Christians who have been justified by faith and whom God has declared righteous and, therefore, not subject to condemnation will be present. Accordingly, the concept many people have that at the judgment seat of Christ people will shed tears because of their misdeeds, or that they will be punished for their failures, is not in keeping with Scripture.

It is significant that all other religions, even Judaism, teach that the individual will be judged according to his works and consequently must do things to gain God's favor. But the New Testament teaches that an individual receives salvation entirely by grace and all our sins were dealt with by Christ's death. For this reason sins will not be an issue at the judgment seat of Christ. The focus will be on what we have attained that is worthwhile.

Several of Paul's illustrations point to the eternal value of living a Christian life. In 1 Corinthians 3:10–15, he compares the Christian life to a building for which Christ is the foundation. The builder has to build on this foundation a building of "gold, silver, precious stones, wood, hay, straw" (v. 12). This building will be tested by fire (v.

13), and what survives the fire will be the basis for reward. Gold, silver, and precious stones will not be consumed by fire, but wood, hay, and stubble will. These materials represent different values and, while this Scripture does not define them, in the Bible gold is used to refer to the glory of God, silver to redemption, and the precious stones to all other things that God may consider worthy. Wood, hay, and straw, obviously, reveal different standards of worth for man, but fire destroys them all because they do not have eternal value.

A second illustration relates the Christian life to a race (1 Cor. 9:24–27). All the factors of successfully running a race are involved, such as, dressing lightly, avoiding anything that would hinder one, starting when the starter says go, staying on the track, not being deterred by anything, and finally winning the crown.

The crowns given in athletic contests in Corinth were made of leaves and were worthless after a few days. But the Christian will get a crown that will not decay. According to verse 25, the Christian's recognition will last forever. In an actual race only one can win, but in the Christian life everyone can win because we will be judged, not by our competition with others, but according to what we do with what God has given us. Even a Christian with very small talents and no significant attainment will win God's "well done" if he uses well what God has provided.

In a third illustration Paul admonishes Christians not to judge each other, but to let God do the judging. In Romans 14:10–12, he uses a figure of stewardship to remind Christians that at the judgment seat of Christ each one will give an accounting of what he did during his lifetime with what God gave him. Of course, the more talent, the more wealth, the more ability for service that an individual Christian receives, so much greater is his responsibility. In the end time he will be required to give an accounting of everything he has done for Christ in proportion to what God gave him to make the service possible.

Accordingly, the judgment seat of Christ is a great corrective to the idea that how a Christian lives makes no difference if he is operating under grace. It is true that what we do during our lives does not affect our salvation if we are genuinely born again, but on the other hand, how we live our lives will affect our rewards. Only those who have served the Lord well will receive a rich reward. Remembering that God will judge us, regardless of how others may define our lives, we can take comfort in 1 Corinthians 4:5: "Then each one's praise will come from God." Even the most obscure Christian who seemingly has accomplished little for God will have something in his life that God will consider worthy of reward.

The subject of rewards is mentioned frequently in Scripture, and often the symbolism of a crown is used to describe it. However, most likely the rewards will be privileged service. The Christian in heaven will be overwhelmed by the wonderful grace and love of God, and he will desire to do something to show his love for God. He will do this by serving. While Scripture is not clear as to how we will serve, in the millennial kingdom we will reign with Christ. In the eternal state, the promise is as recorded in Revelation 22, "His servants shall serve Him" (v. 3). All Christians will receive their just recognition at the judgment seat of Christ. Especially those who have labored in obscurity and sometimes with great sacrifice and fidelity will be rewarded according to their service.

The Fourth Resurrection

Revelation 11:3–13 foretells that God will raise up two witnesses who will bear faithful testimony to Him in the midst of the apostasy that will characterize the world during the end time. They will be prophets who will have the power to bring judgments upon the earth, such as to "shut heaven, so that no rain falls," turn water into blood, and strike the earth with plagues (v. 6). God will protect them from harm (v. 5), and they will testify for 1,260 days.

Then the world ruler will attack and kill the two

witnesses (v. 7) and leave their bodies lying in the streets of Jerusalem (v. 8). After three and a half days, as "those who dwell on the earth . . . rejoice over them" (v. 10), suddenly they will be resurrected and will ascend into heaven in a cloud (vv. 9–11). The event will bring terror to those who watch (v. 11). And God will judge Jerusalem with a severe earthquake that will cause a tenth of the city to collapse and seven thousand people to be killed (v. 13).

Some theologians have interpreted this prophecy as a picture of the Rapture, and others have tried to relate it to either previous or future resurrections. However, the text does not support either view. Perhaps some of the error is due to the statement that the whole world will watch the resurrection and ascension as they occur. Not until the advent of the modern media could the whole world possibly witness an event as it takes place.

Considering the context in which this passage is set and the prophecies that precede and follow it, obviously this passage literally predicts events of the tribulation period. Even though Scripture does not identify the two witnesses, it is probable that they will be of the generation of that time rather than resurrected from a past generation as some scholars have suggested.

The Fifth Resurrection

Revelation 7:9–17 describes a "great multitude which no one could number" (v. 9)—who are "the ones who come out of the great tribulation" (v. 14)—before the throne of God, worshiping Him and serving Him night and day (v. 15).

Revelation 20:4–6 describes the souls of those martyred during the tribulation—"who had not worshiped the beast or his image, and had not received his mark on their foreheads or on their hands" (v. 4)—resurrected and living and reigning "with Christ for a thousand years."

A careful reading of these two passages reveals that they describe the same group of believers—the tribulation dead. The passages that describe other resurrections and judgments make obvious that this "first resurrection" will follow Christ's second coming and will be separated from it by some time. It is not the Rapture, for that event will precede the Second Coming by seven years and will involve only the resurrection of believers of the present age. Nor does this "first resurrection" occur at the Second Coming, for that event is specifically described as Christ coming from heaven to earth accompanied by the saints, His church, who are already resurrected.

The amillennialist attempt to interpret the Chapter 20 passage as describing the new birth of the believers is not supported by the text and actually violates the message of the prophecy. The problem some scholars seem to have with understanding what will happen to the saints of the tribulation, which contributes to their inability to accept the literalism of millennial prophecies, is resolved by the correct understanding of this prophecy concerning this "first resurrection," and in what context it will be the first. Other believers who will die during the tribulation, but who were not martyred, may be resurrected at this time, but Scripture does not specifically discuss their resurrections.

The Sixth Resurrection

According to Daniel 12:1–2 and Isaiah 26:19, the saints of Old Testament times will apparently be raised after the Great Tribulation described by Daniel 11:40–45. Although many scholars have interpreted these prophecies as indicating that the resurrection of Old Testament saints will occur at the rapture of the church, the description of the Rapture is that "the dead in Christ" will be resurrected at that time (1 Thess. 4:16). The expression "in Christ" is a phrase used throughout the New Testament to refer to those baptized by the Spirit. Since being baptized by the Spirit is limited to the church of the present age, which began at Pentecost, it seems that the resurrection of the Old Testament saints will occur not at the Rapture, but after the Second Coming, either before or after the martyred dead of the tribulation are resurrected. Prophecy does not indicate that this occurs on the day of the Second Coming. Most likely it will be a later event.

The Second Judgment

A number of judgments will take place at the time of the Second Coming, including the judgment and destruction of the armies gathered against Christ prophesied in Revelation 19:17–19, the judgment of the beast who is the world ruler and the false prophet, who, according to Revelation 19:20, will be cast into the lake of fire, and the subsequent judgment of everyone, both Gentiles and Jews, who is living at the time.

Matthew 25:31–46 describes in Christ's words the judgment of the nations—the Gentiles. He reveals that after His second coming, His throne will be established on the earth and He will gather before Him all the nations. At that time He will judge individuals rather than political entities. He will designate some as sheep, the saved, and others as goats, the unsaved.

At that time the issue will be whether those living at the time of the Second Coming, who will have survived the Great Tribulation, will be allowed to enter the millennial kingdom. The unsaved will be purged—put to death (Matt. 25:46)—and the righteous will enter the kingdom and receive eternal life (Matt. 25:26). Apparently no adults who are unsaved at the time of the Second Coming will be allowed to enter the millennial kingdom, but no doubt, the many children who have not reached the age of accountability will be admitted.

The finality of this judgment is further developed in Revelation 14, which states that those who received the mark of the beast will live in everlasting punishment (vv. 9–11). These texts are not clear on whether the damned will go immediately into the lake of fire or go first into Hades, which is also a place of fire. However, these passages are clear that the damned will exist for all eternity in the lake of fire.

According to Ezekiel 20:33–38, Israel will be judged in

a similar way. "I will purge the rebels from among you, and those who transgress against Me; I will bring them out of the country where they sojourn, but they shall not enter the land of Israel. Then you will know that I am the LORD" (v. 38). By contrast, those of the nation Israel who are judged to be godly will enter the Promised Land and the millennial kingdom. Numerous passages confirm this, including Ezekiel 39:25–29 and 47:13–48:29. The Gentiles and Israelites who enter the millennial kingdom will do so without rapture, resurrection, or translation; they will enter the kingdom in their natural bodies. This is necessary so that they can populate the earth since the events of the Great Tribulation will have decimated much of the world's population.

During the millennium, the godly survivors of the Great Tribulation will inhabit the earth, with Israel occupying the Promised Land (Isa. 65:18–25). Not only will population increase greatly but apparently death will be postponed. Isaiah 65:20, for example, describes a death at age one hundred as a death in youth. The people will still need houses and will build them and they will also plant crops (65:21–22). Obviously this passage does not describe the present situation or the new heaven and new earth or the new Jerusalem, but the millennial kingdom.

This passage also reveals that Israel will ultimately possess a place in the new heavens and the new earth (v. 17). In other words, Israel has both a millennial hope, which involves the thousand-year kingdom, and an eternal hope, which involves the new Jerusalem and the new heaven and new earth.

All these Scriptures considered together make clear that every believer, whether resurrected or living at the time of the Second Coming, will be judged.

The Final Resurrection and Judgment

According to Revelation 20:11–15, the final judgment will take place in space before a great white throne on which Christ will be seated (v. 11). The dead will stand before Him. Apparently this refers only to the unsaved, as all the righteous will have already been raised. At that time the book in which their deeds are recorded will be opened. If their names are not found in the Book of Life, they will be cast into the lake of fire. Those formerly in Hades, which is a temporary place of the dead, will enter their eternal home, which is described in Revelation 20:14 as the lake of fire and the second death. Because they will be judged according to their works, they will share the eternal destiny of Satan and the fallen angels, for whom the lake of fire was originally created.

Scripture does not describe a resurrection of the saints who will die during the millennium or a rapture of believers who are living at the end of the millennium. However, the assumption that those events will take place seems appropriate.

Understanding this doctrine of final judgment is not an easy matter for Christians. But each must try to comprehend that God is infinite in His righteousness and any sin that is not forgiven is infinite in proportion and requires eternal judgment. The awful fact is that those who will be raised at the final judgment will be given bodies that will continue to be evil and cannot die—bodies that will suffer for all eternity.

Although amillennial theologians tend to merge all the resurrections of Scripture into one general event, careful attention to the details provided by prophetic revelation indicates that those passages reveal no less than seven resurrections which are widely dispersed in time and have differing circumstances. They do not occur at the same time, concern the same people, or even have the same purposes and judgments. The seven are: the resurrection of Christ, the resurrection of a token number of saints following Christ's resurrection, the resurrection of the church at the Rapture, the resurrection of the two tribulation witnesses described in Revelation 11, the resurrection of the tribulation saints, the resurrection of Old Testament saints, and the resurrection of the wicked.

—— 14 ——

THE FOURTEENTH KEY

The Eternal State

Remarkably little attention is given in the Bible to the qualities of eternity. The focus is on truth as it relates to this life and salvation. However, what God reveals in His Word about eternity is quite significant. The most comprehensive revelation of eternity is in Revelation 21 and 22 where we find the prophecy of the new heaven and earth and the new Jerusalem beginning with "Now I saw a new heaven and a new earth, for the first heaven and the first earth had passed away. Also there was no more sea. Then I, John, saw the holy city, New Jerusalem, coming down out of heaven from God, prepared as a bride adorned for her husband" (21:1–2).

The New Heaven and New Earth

The old heaven and earth form the original creation and will continue until the end of the millennial kingdom when the new heaven and earth will be created. The new Jerusalem will replace the earthly Jerusalem, as well as the important city of Babylon, which is described in Revelation 18.

John's introductory description of the new Jerusalem, which compares it to a "bride adorned for her husband," has caused some scholarly debate concerning whether the revelation concerns the bride—the church as a heavenly people—or describes a city. Since a bride is not a city, it seems best to accept the passage as a description of a city

that is beautifully adorned like a bride prepared for marriage. As Revelation 21:9–27 makes clear, the city includes much more than the church. It also includes Israel
and the saved among the Gentiles who are not part of the
church (see Heb. 12:22–24; Rev. 21:12, 14, 24).

Major Features

The introduction of a new heaven and earth and the new
Jerusalem will bring about tremendous change. John's
prophecy describes the blessings this will bring to those
who are saved:

> And I heard a loud voice from heaven saying, "Behold, the
> tabernacle of God is with men, and He will dwell with
> them, and they shall be His people. God Himself will be
> with them and be their God. And God will wipe away every
> tear from their eyes; there shall be no more death, nor
> sorrow, nor crying. There shall be no more pain, for the
> former things have passed away.   (21:3–4)

In contrast to the millennium in which there will be both
sin and death as well as sorrow, the eternal state will be
free of these earthly experiences.

Most expositors agree there will be no death, sorrow, or
pain in the new Jerusalem, but some believe that in
heaven, as saints contemplate the shortcomings of their
lives, there will be tears. Obviously every saint will fall
short. But if regret and sorrow characterize eternity,
heaven would be a miserable place of remorse and self-con-
demnation. Therefore, it is better to conclude that all
these things will be experiences of life before the new
heaven and new earth, rather than something that begins
eternity. Far better is the knowledge that in grace all our
sins are forgiven and God has put them behind us. Our
eternal emotion will be thankfulness and worship rather
than grief for our earthly experiences. This point of view
seems to be confirmed by the statement, "for the former
things have passed away."

The concept of grace is difficult for man who is so geared
to earning his rewards. In fact, all religions except Christianity teach that eternal salvation will be based on

earthly works. But the Bible teaches that salvation is entirely of grace and a work of God in spite of the unworthiness of the recipients. Remorse and sorrow will be foreign to heaven as this world passes away forever. The reason for rejoicing is in the words of the One seated on the throne, who says, "Behold, I make all things new" (21:5).

John was so astounded by the revelation of what he saw and heard, he had to be instructed to, "Write, for these words are true and faithful." The one who makes these pronouncements is obviously Jesus Christ, "the Alpha and the Omega, the Beginning and the End" (v. 6). And He gives a reminder that salvation is the gift of God to those who will trust in Him: "To him who is thirsty I will give to drink without cost from the spring of the water of life" (v. 6 NIV).

Those described as "overcomers" will receive the promise of eternal life and the blessings of a new heaven and earth (v. 7 NIV). This expression does not distinguish some believers from others, but is a description of all who triumph by faith in Christ. In contrast, the destiny of unbelievers, because of their rejection of God's grace, is "the fiery lake of burning sulfur" which is "the second death" (v. 8 NIV).

The introductory presentation of the new heaven and new earth and the new Jerusalem describes a new creation. The Greek term for constructing something, *poeo*, as well as the word for *create, ktizo,* both appear in this passage, along with the Greek word for *new, kainos.* The use of these terms emphasizes that an entirely new situation is described. This is in keeping with the destruction of the heaven and earth which will have "passed away" (21:1). Second Peter 3:10 and 12, reveal that the earth will be "burned up" by fire and "the elements will melt with fervent heat." Thus God will eventually destroy the world which He created.

John's description of the new Jerusalem "coming down out of heaven from God" (21:2) has raised the question of whether it will be in existence during the millennial kingdom, since this prophecy does not describe the new Jerusalem being created at this time.

Though there is little evidence in Scripture to support the concept, possibly the new Jerusalem will be a satellite city above the earth during the millennium. Obviously, it will not rest on the millennial earth. If it is a satellite city, it could conceivably be the residence of the resurrected and translated saints who could commute to earth to carry on their earthly functions. They could do this much as a person does who lives in the country and commutes to a city office in our present life. Strangely enough, none of the millennial passages picture a person still in his natural body living next to a person who is in his resurrection body. Therefore, the theory of a satellite city would seem to fit. However, this is not something that should be dogmatically held, as scriptural revelation is insufficient.

Some amillenarians who attempt to find a place for fulfillment of millennial passages have tried to find the millennial kingdom in the new heaven and earth. However, the two periods are quite different. They are different not only in the ways revealed in the book of Revelation, but in their character as well. Some people are confused by references to the new Jerusalem in passages that are basically about the millennium (see Isa. 65:17; 66:22; 2 Peter 3:13; Rev. 3:12). However, discussing in a passage future events that are widely different is a common characteristic of the Bible. Therefore, the argument that references in a particular passage must all refer to the same entity is not valid. Often, for example, the Old Testament speaks of the first and second comings of Christ in the same verse without mentioning the time period between these two events (see Isa. 61:1–2). Scripture reveals that in the new heaven and earth there will be no sin, no judgment, no death, no geographic landmarks of the kind we have in our present world, no ocean, no vegetation apart from the tree of life, and so forth. These characteristics will not be true of the millennial kingdom.

The New Jerusalem

Beginning with Revelation 21:9, John describes the new Jerusalem as "the bride, the Lamb's wife." As stated before, although there has been scholarly debate on this point, the preferable interpretation is to regard the description of the city as meaning a literal city that is as beautifully adorned as a bride, rather than trying to suggest the symbolism of a bride who is represented by a city.

The city will be like a gigantic jewel, a "jasper stone, clear as crystal" (v. 11). The jasper we know today is an opaque jewel, but in biblical description this jewel and others mentioned in prophecy of the future often take on different characteristics from those most common to the jewels we know in this life.

Major Features

A wall, 144 cubits high, will surround the city (v. 17). (The NIV translates this dimension as "thick," but that is unwarranted. The preferable translation is "height.") If a cubit equals eighteen inches, the wall will be 216 feet high. The significance of the wall is that it can exclude those who are unworthy of being in the city. However, the wall has three gates on each of its four sides. This indicates access to and exodus from the city. The fact that the gates are described as east, north, south, and west supports the idea that the new earth will be round, although the city itself will be square.

The names of Israel are on the twelve gates. These may be arranged in the same order as in the millennial temple and the gates of the earthly Jerusalem, as recorded in Ezekiel 48:31–34. The fact of the twelve gates focuses attention on many other descriptions that involve the number twelve, such as twelve tribes, twelve angels, and twelve foundations (vv. 12–14). In addition, the text describes twelve pearls (v. 21) and twelve kinds of fruit (22:2). Furthermore the city's height, length, and width are each 12,000 furlongs, or stadia. These dimensions usually are considered to be roughly the equivalent of

1,500 miles, if a furlong is exactly ten feet. Therefore, the new Jerusalem will be a tremendous city, much larger than anything mankind has ever known on earth. Obviously, it will not be resting on the earth in the millennium.

Debate continues on whether the city is a cube or a pyramid, although the evidence seems to favor a pyramid shape, inasmuch as the water from the throne at the top of the city flows down its sides (22:1). The description says the entire wall will be made of jasper, like a gigantic jewel, and the city itself of "pure gold, like clear glass" (21:18).

Theologically significant is the fact that the foundations of the city will have the names of the twelve apostles (21:14). Both the names of Israel and the names of the apostles appearing in the city indicate that both Israel and the church will be involved, although some have tried to limit the new Jerusalem to only the church. However, Revelation 21:24 states, "And the nations of those who are saved shall walk in its light, and the kings of the earth bring their glory and honor into it," indicating that all who are saved will be present, not just those of the church of the present age known otherwise as the body of Christ. That all the saved will be included in the city is further verified by the revelation of Hebrews 12:22–24:

> But you have come to Mount Zion and to the city of the living God, the heavenly Jerusalem, to an innumerable company of angels, to the general assembly and church of the firstborn who are registered in heaven, to God the Judge of all, to the spirits of just men made perfect, to Jesus the Mediator of the new covenant, and to the blood of sprinkling that speaks better things than that of Abel.

This passage makes clear that all the saints—"the spirits of just men made perfect"—not just the church of the present age, as well as Jesus Himself, will be in the city.

The foundations of the city will be made of various jewels, each having its own characteristic and embracing every color of the rainbow (Rev. 21:19–20). The gates of the wall will be huge pearls. They will not be natural pearls as we know them today, but will look like pearls (v. 21). Even the gold in the city will not correspond to gold as we know it today. It is described as "like transparent glass" (v. 21). Apparently all the materials of the new Jerusalem, including the jewels and the gold, will be translucent and the glory of God, which is the light of the city, will shine through them. The glory of God will be such that "the nations will walk by its light, and the kings of the earth will bring their splendor into it. On no day will its gates ever be shut, for there will be no night there" (vv. 24–25 NIV). The city itself will constitute a temple to God (v. 22), and God will make it His temple.

Revelation 22 gives additional details of the "river of the water of life," which will flow from the throne of God, apparently from the top of the city down its sloping walls, and through the middle of the great street (vv. 1–2 NIV). Verse 2 indicates that the tree of life will be "on either side of the river." Apparently it will be either a huge tree whose branches span the river or there will be multiple trees on each side. The tree of life will bear twelve crops, yielding fruit every month (v. 2). This is a reminder that the tree of life found in the Garden of Eden (Gen. 3:22) and forbidden to Adam and Eve, will be in the eternal state as the common possession of the saints of God.

Some confusion has risen from the statement, "The leaves of the tree were for the healing of the nations" (v. 2). Some theologians have suggested that this portion of Scripture is retrospective and actually describes the millennial situation, because no healing will be necessary in the eternal state. However, a different interpretation would be justified, indicating that the healing is for the "health" of the nations and may be connected somehow to their eternal well-being physically. Other characteristics of the new Jerusalem seem to make trying to fit it into the millennial situation impossible.

Many questions arise concerning the role of the saints in the new heaven and earth and the new Jerusalem. Their role is summarized in the statement, "And there shall be no more curse, but the throne of God and of the Lamb shall be in it, and His servants shall serve Him.

They shall see His face, and His name shall be on their foreheads" (vv. 3–4). Although Scripture does not reveal much concerning the role and activities of saints in eternity, the simple statement, "His servants shall serve Him," seems to describe it well. The supreme desire of every saint in eternity will be to express love and obedience to Christ, and this will be in keeping with service for God.

Apparently there will be no need for sleep or rest in the eternal state as there will be no night and no need for the light of the sun or moon (21:25; 22:5).

Eternity

The Bible reveals that heaven will go on forever (Rev. 22:5). The unsaved will be excluded and the righteous included—*forever*.

The book of Revelation closes with a renewed invitation for those living in our present world to hear the Gospel and respond, and to "take the water of life freely" (22:17). It also reminds us all that Christ will be coming soon (v. 20).

Although the description of heaven found in Revelation 21 and 22 is augmented slightly in other passages, such as Isaiah 65:17; 66:22; and 2 Peter 3:10–13, remarkably something so important has only brief reference in Scripture. The reason is, of course, that Scripture was written to help us live our lives on earth in keeping with God's will. The vision of the future is sufficiently enticing to encourage us in our earthly walk with the prospect of being in the presence of the Lord forever.

And that is what eternity will be—forever.

The book of Revelation reveals our eternal destiny and our eternal home. In these pages God describes the blessings His children will receive throughout eternity, blessings that will eclipse all the sorrows and struggles of this life. He challenges us anew to faith and comprehension of His incomparable grace extended to those who put their trust in Christ.

No other book of the Bible presents more clearly the blessedness of the saints and the utter misery of the

wicked. Yet many people pass by the blessings of Scripture and faith in Christ, drifting through life without
availing themselves of what God has provided by grace
through Jesus Christ.

Revelation is a book to be read and studied carefully.
But probably it is the most neglected book of the New
Testament, deemed too confusing to be understood and
ruled out as an effective revelation of God. Some even
have labeled it fiction.

No work of fiction could possibly equal the tremendous
revelation of this book, presenting as it does the glory and
majesty of God, His sovereignty, power, righteousness,
and omniscience, as well as the indescribable glories of
what He has in store for each one of His children.

It is fitting to close this brief study of prophecy by
quoting the final verses of Revelation. They follow John's
testimony that he faithfully and accurately set down the
revelation shown to him of "the things which must shortly
take place," the angel's assurance that "these words are
faithful and true" (22:6), and a warning.

> The Spirit and the bride say, "Come!" And let him who
> hears say, "Come!" And let him who thirsts come. And
> whoever desires, let him take the water of life freely. For
> I testify to everyone who hears the words of the prophecy
> of this book: If anyone adds to these things, God will add
> to him the plagues that are written in this book; and if
> anyone takes away from the words of the book of this
> prophecy, God shall take away his part from the Book of
> Life, from the holy city, and from the things which are
> written in this book.
>
> He who testifies to these things says, "*Surely I am
> coming quickly.*"
>
> Amen. Even so, come, Lord Jesus!   (Rev. 22:17–20)

Those who have trusted Christ as they face the problems of this life have the blessed assurance that Christ is
coming again and echo John's prayer: Come, Lord Jesus!

SUBJECT INDEX

SCRIPTURE INDEX

8:32	97	4:4	99	2:13	114
8:34	29, 99	4:7–16	100	3:5	45
9—11	14	4:8–10	107	**Hebrews**	
9:11	34	4:11–16	99	1:3	99
11:1	14	4:12–16	99	1:10–12	26
11:25–26	31	4:5–16	99	2:14	25, 28
11:25–27	14	4:20–24	101	4:13	8
12:1	97	4:30	94	5:5	28
12:3–8	99, 100	5:18	46	7:3	28
14:10–12	160	5:23	100	7:15–17	31
14:11	21	5:25	93	7:20–21	98
1 Corinthians		5:26	101	7:23–25	31
3:10–15	159	5:27	101	7:24	98
3:11–17	97	5:30	99	7:25	28, 29, 94, 97, 98, 99
3:12	160	**Philippians**		7:27	99
3:13	160	1:23	103, 107	8:8	45, 86
4:5	161	2:13	7	9:11–12	97
5:6–8	91	3:21	26, 111	9:12	99
6:19	46	**Colossians**		9:15	45, 86
6:19–20	94	1:14	94	9:24	29
8:7	37	1:16	26	10:5	25
9:24–27	160	1:17	26	10:19–22	98
9:25	160	1:24	99	11:7	37
11:25	45, 86	2:9	27	12:1	111
12:4–28	99	2:19	99, 100	12:22–24	168, 172
12:12–14	100	3:1–3	94	13:8	26
12:13	46, 94	3:11	101	13:12	99
12:27–28	100	3:13	27	13:15–16	29, 97
15:3–4	157	4:12	98	**James**	
15:24–28	21, 29	**1 Thessalonians**		5:7–8	31
15:51–52	111	1:10	110	**1 Peter**	
15:51–58	32, 158	2:19	110	1:10–11	60
15:53	111	3:13	110	1:20	34
15:58	159	4:13	110	2:5	29
2 Corinthians		4:13–14	135	2:5–6	97
3:6	45, 86	4:13–18	32, 135, 158	5:8	143
3:6–18	82	4:14	158, 110	5:9	144
3:11	82	4:15–17	111	**2 Peter**	
3:15–18	82	4:16	163	1:20–21	9
5:1–5	107	4:16–18	102	2:1	90
5:8	107	4:17	158	2:1–22	91
5:10	159	4:18	114	2:4	64
5:10–11	117	5	114, 115	2:6	64
5:17	94, 101	5:1	114	3:3–4	31, 91
11:2	101	5:3	123	3:10	169
11:14	67, 137	5:4	128	3:10–13	174
15:51–52	158	**2 Thessalonians**		3:12	169
Galatians		2:1–4	115	3:13	170
2:16	43	2:1–12	92	5:8	137
3:21–22	43	2:3	59, 115, 116	**1 John**	
3:24–25	42	2:3–4	122	2:1	94
3:27–28	101	2:4	59	2:15–17	91
4:24–26	82	2:7–8	116	2:18	92, 122
4:28	82	2:8	31	2:22	92
4:30	82	**1 Timothy**		4:3	122
6:15	101	2:1	98	**2 John**	
Ephesians		2:5	28	1:7	92, 122
1:4–5	33	4:1	90	**Jude**	
1:11	33	4:1–2	37	1:14–15	31, 138
1:13–14	46	4:2–3	90	**Revelation**	
1:19–23	94	6:14–15	31	1:1	20
1:22–23	100	**2 Timothy**		1:7–8	31
1:23	99	1:9	34	1:8	26
2:7	94	4:1	27	1:18	27
2:14–16	101	4:2–3	90	2:12–17	55
2:15–16	99			2:19	26
2:19–22	97	**Titus**			
3:6	99	1:2	34		
3:11	34				

About the Author

Dr. John F. Walvoord is Chancellor of Dallas Theological Seminary, where he was a member of the Theology Faculty from 1936 until 1986, president from 1952 until 1986, and editor of *Bibliotheca Sacra* from 1952 until 1986. He is one of the leading conservative evangelical theologians of America and is a specialist in the field of biblical eschatology. He holds the A.B. and D.D. degrees from Wheaton College; the A.M. from Texas Christian University; the Th.B., Th.M., and Th.D. from Dallas Theological Seminary; and the Litt.D. from Liberty Baptist Seminary.

In addition to numerous articles published in *Bibliotheca Sacra*, Dr. Walvoord has written for *Moody Monthly*, *Christianity Today*, and other Christian publications. Over three million copies of his books are in print, including *Armageddon, Oil and the Middle East Crisis, What We Believe: Discovering the Truths of Scripture*, and *Major Bible Prophecies*. His first book, *The Holy Spirit*, published in 1943, is still in distribution.

Dr. Walvoord and his wife, Geraldine, are the parents of three adult children and live in Dallas, Texas.